MW01232122

Finding Fresh Passion to Worship

By Igho Lewis Yegbeburu

PRESS

Copyright © 2011 by Igho Lewis Yegbeburu

Finding Fresh Passion To Worship
by Igho Lewis Yegbeburu

Printed in the United States of America

ISBN 9781612157627

All rights reserved solely by the author. The author guarantees all contents are original and do not infringe upon the legal rights of any other person or work. No part of this book may be reproduced in any form without the permission of the author. The views expressed in this book are not necessarily those of the publisher.

Unless otherwise indicated, Bible quotations are taken from The Amplified® Bible. Copyright © 1954, 1958, 1962, 1964, 1965, 1987 by The Lockman Foundation. Used by permission; The King James Version (KJV) of the Holy Bible; The New American Standard Bible® (NASB). Copyright © 1960, 1962, 1963, 1968, 1971, 1972, 1973, 1977, 1995 by The Lockman Foundation. Used by permission; The HOLY BIBLE, NEW INTERNATIONAL VERSION®. NIV®. Copyright © 1973, 1978, 1984 by International Bible Society. Used by permission of Zondervan; and The *Holy Bible,* New Living Translation (NLT). Copyright © 1996 by Tyndale House Publishers, Inc., Wheaton, Illinois, 60189. Used by permission.

www.xulonpress.com

DEDICATION

This book is dedicated to the giver and sustainer of life, my Savior and Master, Jesus Christ. Through His infinite mercies, He chose to use me for His praise and glory. It was by His stirring of my soul that I was able to both contemplate and articulate the insights shared in this book. And to Jesus be all the praise and glory.

ACKNOWLEDGMENT

〰

This book is not without the influence and contribution of many upon my life and ministry. These divine vessels over many years made tremendous deposits upon me directly or indirectly. Only eternity will be able to reveal the actual degree of impartation several books, audio and videotapes, or CDs made in my life. This also includes the various Bible studies, discipleship courses, seminars, and seminary classes which were thought-provoking and spiritually inspiring in shaping my understanding about worship.

I will not fail to acknowledge by name some individuals without whom the ideas shared in this book would have been too elusive. They include: Billy Graham, Charles Swindoll, A W Tozer, Ayo Oritsejafor, Benny Hinn, Kathryn Kuhlman, R.W. Schambach, John Osteen, Joel Osteen, Rev. Dr. Paul O. Davidson, Oral Roberts, Pat Robertson, T.D Jakes, Reinhard Bonnke, Myles Munroe, Bishop Noel Jones, Rick Warren, Matthew Ashimolowo, Tommy Tenny, Evangelist Job Alabi, Dr. T. Leigh, Pastor E.A Adeboye, Bishop David Oyedepo, Bishop Dickson Olorunda, Rev. Chika Ossai, Claude V. King, Henry Blackaby, Prophet Kobus van Rensburg, John Hagee, Rev. Thomas Anyanhun, Bob Fitts, Morris Chapman, Clint Brown, Phil Driscoll, Ron Kenoly, Don Moen, Shirley Caesar, Donnie McClurkin, Michael W. Smith, Israel Houghton, Darlene Zschech, Byron Cage, Kevin Bond, Panam P. Paul, Rev. Fred

Ozegbe, Maranatha! Singers, Integrity Music, Hillsong Music, my seminary lecturers, and a host of others.

Worthy of mentioning is the executive producer of The Glorious Fountain Ministries, Austin E. Oghenejobo, our board of trustees, and friends and members of The Glorious Fountain Ministries from various nations around the globe who are on the front line with me to promote intimate and passionate worship to the praise and glory of our God. Our love for the Lord has brought us this far as we labor together to build up passionate worshippers for the kingdom of our God. You mean so much to me.

Finally, I am forever grateful to God for my wife and faithful friend, Toyin, and our kids—David, Sharon, and Bliss—for provoking me to deeper dimensions of worship by their willingness to run with the vision and their invaluable sacrifice in standing with me to fulfill the ministry. I love you all. Thanks and God bless.

CONTENTS

PREFACE

❧

The decision to write this book was not born out of a desire to write, it was birthed by a continuous burden which came upon me week in and out as I observed that much of what is called worship in most religious houses is a far cry from the yearning of desperate souls seeking to encounter God.

So much seems to be happening but only very little impart is being made. What most churches label "worship" are actually lifeless and passive routines that have been passed from one generation to another.

Other worship routines may be just a few years old but are obviously lacking in the ability to satisfy the simple yearning of the parishioners. Some others seem to be in a kind of limbo, lacking consistency. On a particular day the worship experience may be heavenly, but on the next people leave disappointed because what they have experienced does not qualify to be called worship.

Churches are seeing many who were once denominational devotees abandoning their religious roots for something far from their traditions and doctrine of many years. In some cases, almost a whole generation has relocated because there seems to be nothing relevant to them going on there.

Finding Fresh Passion to Worship is not designed to be an academic resource with lots of definitions and research work to verify the issues raised. Rather it is the content of the heart of a worshipper who is burdened to see God's people encounter

God in an ever-increasing degree of glory. It is an attempt to answer the salient questions in the hearts of millions who are hungry and thirsty for an encounter with God. They are not in search of a plan or method. They just want to find the answer to the yearnings of their soul, and this is only evident in an unquestionable impartation that is beyond words.

The challenge from one church to the other may differ, but the needs of the souls of mankind remain the same everywhere. As it is with the mighty so it is with the lowly; they both have a yearning for God in their inmost being.

The astronomical transformations taking place in our ever changing world make our religious routines and traditions look like a joke to the watching world. Scientists, by their discoveries and technological breakthroughs, continually hold the world in amazement as they unfold to the entire human race the next level of our advancement. By the propounding of theories and hypotheses, many have been challenged to undertake extensive and expensive research, believing they can be counted among those making a meaningful change in our world. But it is sad to observe that in the church only a few people are passionate enough to seek for the much needed manifestation of the glory that provokes a sense of reverential awe in people.

When our worship experience is devoid of the reverential awe, fascination, and divine manifestations that lead to transformed lives, we lose relevance in our dynamic world.

So much competes for the attention of man, and if we lack that which is fascinating enough to compel people to contemplate worship, we are likely to lose them to something else. This is why you can find people who believe in science but don't believe in God. When they came to church, they saw lifeless religious routine, but when they entered the arena of science their minds were mesmerized by things they could not easily fathom. But the truth is that there is much more fascination in worship than in science or any other realm of life.

I am confident this book will not only open the eyes of the reader to the truth about worship, it will also enhance and revive our individual worship experience and by extension transform the worship life of small groups and churches.

I believe a mighty revival is coming to our world and that worship renewal has been orchestrated to play a significant role in this great move of the Spirit of God. I am convinced that our God is about to manifest Himself in the most unlikely places through the most unlikely vessels, and when this begins to happen the world will see the glory and power of the Lord like never before.

We are about to see more warehouses and abandoned industrial buildings converted to places of worship as this river of God stirs up a fresh passion to worship all over the world.

As you encounter God in the course of this journey, may you begin to grow in your intimacy with the Lord till worship becomes a sweet response from your inmost being to the lover of your soul. Shalom!

INTRODUCTION

THE CRY FROM WITHIN

The gathering of men and women in various religious groups all over the world week after week accounts for the greatest regular gathering of souls compared to entertainment and sports put together.

Churches, mosques, synagogues, temples, and shrines the world over enjoy such huge patronage that it makes one wonder: why such devotion? If such devotions alone account for righteousness and peace, our world would have become a better place for all.

Instead, it has become obvious that devotion to religious form does not translate into true satisfaction of the soul. So many people travel the earth from one pilgrimage to the other in hope of experiencing a new dimension to their faith, but after a while they still have to wander in search of the answer. Many have had reasons to cross from one religious group to another in pursuit of a better spiritual experience only to end up despondent and unfulfilled.

When a man is hungry, he does not need a prophet or a soothsayer to name his problem or predict his steps. From within his being there will be enough signals to order his steps. His nose suddenly becomes extra sensitive to the smell of food in the air, and he begins to salivate. If he refuses to comply with the yearning of his body, his stomach will start to rumble and sometimes loudly enough to embarrass the individual. If he still chooses to ignore all of these signals, after a while a slight pain will commence in the head. By this time he may experience loss of coordination and clear reasoning. This is when he is compelled to listen to the voice of reasoning, and the only reasonable thing to do to avert this degenerating into a serious breakdown is to follow the path that leads to a plate of food and water.

Everyone can accurately interpret and follow the signal that calls for the restoration of the lost energy of the body, but not everyone has been able to discern and accurately follow after that which leads to the restoration of the spirit.

The body is natural and earthly, so it is normal for it to be sensitive to its natural environment and resources. But the spirit of man is not natural or earthly. It belongs to another realm. Therefore, it can never be nourished by natural or earthly resources.

From Genesis 2:7, we see that the source of the body of man is the earth (humus), so it is acceptable to rejuvenate it by that which proceeds from the earth. Therefore, man can return to the earth (humus) to meet the need of the body (resourcing the body through food). But the source of the spirit of man is not the earth, it is from the Father of life—it is the impartation of the breath and life of God (Genesis 1:26-27, 2:7b). It is therefore unacceptable and inappropriate to rejuvenate the spirit by earthly options.

David, the great king and prophet of Israel, once said, "He makes me lie down in green pastures, he leads me beside quiet waters, he restores my soul."[1]

There is a place where the soul of man is nourished and renewed. It is a realm far from the physical. When King David spoke of his soul being restored, he made use of a word which gives us a clue that the restoration he spoke of took place in his invisible spiritual being.

The natural realm is a strange realm to the soul of man. The spirit of man is like a fish out of water in the natural realm. The more it dwells in the natural realm, the more it struggles to stay alive. The only way the spirit is able to triumph in this realm is when it is continually rejuvenated by a firm connection to its true source. This is the reason why from within each soul there is this struggle to return and reconnect with its original source. When a soul is able to find this place, like David, it will experience true restoration. This is the reason why the fellowship between the first man Adam and the source of life was so imperative.

Deep down from the inmost being of every soul is this gentle but importunate desire designed to reconnect us to our source. It is like a spiritual GPS implant, carefully designed by the source of our spirit to help bring us to our destination, restoring us to the place where our soul is nourished to live out the abundant life.

The craving for that which is out of the ordinary in the soul of every man is an indication of the soul's yearning to become acquainted with the true source of life.

Limited by a mindset that is more at home with the fallen nature, the spirit of man continually groans to become reunited and rejuvenated by the source and owner of our souls. The soul can sense it far away and knows that it is possible to reach out to this source, yet every effort seems to be elusive. Bewildered by the clamor of the flesh, so many people find it hard to locate the way. After several attempts, many have settled for that which is a far cry from the true passion of their souls, and not long afterward they discover it lacked that sense of eternal peace and the satisfaction of life beyond the physical which they truly desire.

It's Not by Might

So many try to take solace in philosophy, religious rituals, and certain organizations but soon discover it has not met the craving of their souls. By the time they get to the pinnacle of their obsession, it only reveals how empty the whole thing has been, and like a mirage it disappears when it seems to be within their reach.

Alexander the Great is said to be the only military commander undefeated in his expeditions around the world. He was so fierce and powerful in battle that he was able to conquer the various oppositions of his time. But after he conquered the whole world, it was said that he began to weep. Why would a man weep after conquering the world? There was no more world to be added to his domain.

How can a man have the whole world and still feel empty? It's simply because it was the end of an obsession, the end of an exercise in futility. Any accomplishment devoid of the true longing of our spirits will always leave in us a feeling of dissatisfaction and vainness.

When men come to the end of all their achievements, it suddenly dawns on them that the true need of their souls is spiritual. In search of this answer, many have become religious. Unfortunately, the answer is not in man's devotion to any religious form. A religious form may have a form of godliness but be devoid of the power that brings true joy and a sense of fulfillment that is eternal (2 Timothy 3:5).

Mere religious form does not have the power to connect people to the true source. Religious people have correctly sensed that the path that leads to the restoration of their soul is worship, but the problem is that such worship—hinging upon how much they are able to do in their devotion to rules, regulations, and rituals—is very inadequate. This in itself is a big mistake, but a greater mistake is for one to call such unfortunate and fruitless pursuit worship.

That which is unable to quench the thirst of the soul is not qualified to be called worship. If it is simply rules and regulations without a divine intimate relationship that transforms the soul, it is not worship. If it leaves one more bewildered and unfulfilled, it is not worship. If it only helps you to escape from your troubles for a while, it is not worship. If the reason one is devoted to such endless rituals is to avoid the anger of a particular deity, it is not worship. From a distance it may look so real and tangible, but upon a stronger and closer observation it is nothing but a great delusion.

If it were true worship, it would nourish the worshipper and sustain him/her in a relationship saturated with peace, love, and joy.

There Is a Mediator

Many continue to struggle because they have ignored or considered irrational the atonement of the one who is the way, the truth, and the life.

He is the only begotten of the Father of our spirits. He is called the door. Why? Because He is the only one who can usher us into the presence of the Father of our spirits. His name is Jesus Christ of Nazareth. He proceeded from the Father and He alone can bring us to the Father.

The Father is the one who formed man out of the dust of the earth, and when He breathed the breath of life into man's nostrils, he (the dust) became a living soul; this is the first Adam (Genesis 2:7).

The Father is the true source of the soul of man, and He is the one the inmost being of man seeks to reconnect and have communion with.

This struggle to return to the source only became necessary after the first Adam fell out of fellowship with the Father by the disobedience that led to his spiritual death (Genesis 3). But by the sacrificial death of the second Adam (Christ), who was the breath of God deposited in and born of a virgin (Luke 1:27-35), we now have eternal redemption. He is the true mediator between the Father and mankind (Ephesians 2:13-14). The good news is that by the atonement of Christ, we have been given the Holy Spirit as an assurance of a continuous connectivity and communion with the Father, who is the true source of our spirits (Ephesians 1:10-14). By this a soul can live in this house called a body and also experience the life of the spirit on earth.

The inherent drive for a better understanding to the true meaning and purpose of life in each soul cannot be satisfied by the vain philosophies of mortal man. Many among those considered the great minds and leaders of their generations have carried out extensive studies and observations hoping to proffer solutions to this problem, only to end up with mere philosophies and theories that further compound the problem of man.

Spiritual problems can only be satisfied by the true identification of the source of life and a return to the Father of our spirits.

There Is a Connection to the Source

The presence of the various religious houses all over the world indicates the effort of man to help connect to the source. But more often than not most religious houses have only compounded the frustration of man by their undue emphasis on sectional theology, doctrine, rites, and the like.

Most religious folks actually went in search of the substance but ended up with the shadow (a mere religious form). To mistake religious form for worship is to accept the shadow as the substance.

For any soul to locate the true substance, it must be willing and ready to follow the fervor of the soul to its true source. By the desperation in our souls, God has placed in us a guide to help us navigate our way to true worship.

The communion we lost in the nature we inherited from the fallen Adam we now have restored to us in the nature of the second Adam. "So it is written: 'The first man Adam became a living being'; the last Adam, a life-giving spirit....As was the earthly man so are those who are of the earth; and as is the man from heaven, so are those who are of heaven."[2]

It is by reason of our union with Christ that we have been raised together with Christ and are made to sit with Him in the heavenly realm (Ephesians 2:6). In the spirit of the new creation, we are able to soar to limitless heights as we express the joy of our glorious liberty in Christ in deep communion and worship that is exhilarating and passionate.

Only after the fall of the first Adam did it become a difficult task for man to truly and quickly identify the yearning of his spirit. Before the fall it was not so.

CHAPTER ONE

REMINISCENCES OF THE FIRST ENCOUNTER

Before the fall, the voice and presence of God in the garden was the joy and satisfaction of man's desire. Man could not wait to enjoy the loving embrace of the Father. Each encounter with the Father was the most exciting and blissful experience of the day. The encounter, no matter how long, seemed but a few minutes. Adam was continually fascinated by the awesomeness of God's presence and glory. Lost in deep admiration of his maker and Father, he would lie there prostrate in worship. His soul was flabbergasted by the glory of the Father, who loved him so dearly He created him in His own image and likeness. And to know that the Father had made him the crown of his magnificent creation was an honor too hard to imagine, but it was real.

Adam could see that the beauty and glory from the Father which surrounded and overwhelmed him could be found in no other in heaven or on earth. In such moments of fellowship, every touch from the Father was an impartation of unfathomable ecstasy and power. Every word imparted power, wisdom, knowledge, and understanding. Through this glorious fellowship the being of man was overwhelmed by divine light, and as his spirit communed with the Spirit of the Father, he became flooded with divine insight.

It was in such moments of deep intimacy and communion that the Father proffered answers to satisfy the curiosity of this man born into the glory and wealth of the everlasting Father. There was just too much for his mind to fathom. The mystery of the Everlasting One and the happenings of the dateless past and the unknown future would take quite a lot to comprehend. That notwithstanding, he made progress and before long exceeded the angelic beings in the understanding of mysteries.

Though the angelic beings had access to God's presence and were therefore overwhelmed with divine truth as they bowed in worship, none of them had such fellowship and intimacy with the Almighty. This is why moments like this became so precious to the angelic beings: it offered them the rare privilege of gaining insight into the Almighty's purpose, plans, and personality. The angels witnessed this intimate fellowship between man and his heavenly Father (Ephesians 3:9-12). It also gave them a better understanding of life and the laws and governance of the universe.

For Adam, there was just too much to comprehend in each divine encounter with the Ancient of Days. Each glimpse of His face was an electrifying and awe-inspiring encounter that overwhelmed every fiber of Adam's being, causing him to cry out in reverential awe.

It would not be too hard to imagine that the Lord often left while Adam was still basking in the joy of this moment, awe-struck and overwhelmed by the avalanche of love that flowed from the Father and now filled his heart as he lay prostrate on the ground.

It is in such encounters that we find the true motivation to worship with fresh passion. In this place, worship is not by some sense of duty; it has become the much needed living water to quench the thirst of the soul. And what a joy and satisfaction to have our souls nourished by the glorious fountain from above. This is abundant life and peace.

To the human soul, nothing in the whole world can be compared to this encounter. True worship is not done out of necessity or duty; it is an encounter with much delight and expectancy.

But when Adam fell, it became the greatest gloom and sadness you can ever imagine. Artists and poets can never accurately express the degree of darkness, disappointment, and misery that engulfed all of creation the day man fell. He who had the rare privilege to enter into a glorious encounter with the Father at the cool of the day became disoriented and estranged from the lover and joy of his soul (Genesis 3:8-10).

It became a struggle to gain access into such moments of intimate fellowship that were once his blissful abode and domain, and this is how the great search began.

Man, a Desperate Being

The growing discontent and endless pursuits of many today are only a reflection of the emptiness of man outside God.

Man's alienation from an intimate fellowship with the Father by the corruption of sin made him mentally and spiritually disoriented. This is the reason why the soul of man is always in search of something more. And no one will be able to lay hold of this yearning except it is revealed by the Spirit. Those who have been able to gain access back to this place of divine intimacy all have one thing in common: they have established a personal relationship and fellowship with the Father through the Son, Jesus.

After the fall and through the period of the old covenant, only a few persons like Enoch, Abraham, and Moses had intimate fellowship with God until the atonement of the Messiah was accomplished.

For such, their hunger for that intimate fellowship with the Father was a passion strong enough to make them go an extra mile. This desire for a glorious time with the Lord was a longing to hear His voice, feel His touch, and enjoy His presence.

Such is the passion we find expressed in songs like "In the Garden." Just reading through the lines of this song will reveal to you the passion in the heart of a desperate worshipper.

I come to the garden alone When the dew is still on the roses; And the voice I hear, falling on my ear The Son of God discloses
Chorus:
And He walks with me and He talks with me And He tells me I am His own. And the joy we share as we tarry there, None other has ever known.[1]

Enthralled by a Glorious Hush

There is something beyond description about the manifest presence of the Lord. When He shows up, without a word, He is able to communicate so much to our souls. But when He does speak, it is always too beautiful and glorious to describe. His words are so powerful they reach deep down to every fiber of our being. The hosts of heaven and earth have to be in a perfect hush to comprehend what He has to say.

In stanza two of the song "In the Garden," we have it well expressed with the following words: "He speaks and the sound of His voice is so sweet the birds hush their singing, and the melody that He gave to me within my heart is ringing."[2]

It is in such intimate and glorious encounter with the lover of our souls that we find the fresh passion to worship again and again. If you know what this is all about you will not want to miss a moment of this encounter. You will yearn to experience every bit of it.

Pastor E.A. Adeboye of The Redeemed Christian Church of God once said, "The reason Peter was able to catch many fishes when the Lord Jesus told him to let down the nets (after he toiled all night catching nothing), is because the fishes came to hear the voice of Jesus."[3] I love the idea that they came to hear the voice of Jesus.

Until you learn to quiet your flesh, you are not ready to pick up the wavelength of the Spirit. To hear His voice is to receive life for your soul. When you truly know Him, He becomes the very breath you need to live.

For those who know this life, it is not hard to imagine why Clint Brown wrote the song "Breathe on Me" the way he did.

(More details of the lyrical content of this song can be found in the album *Give God the Highest Praise*).

Any soul that has encountered the intimate fellowship of God's presence can truly testify that there is no alternative. The more you have of Him, the better you are sure to become in every sense of life and godliness. Your confidence will rise to a new level, and in no time you will soar on the wings of the Spirit to a new realm of worship. This is where the soul is ushered into a place of deep communion with the Father and we are able to say with the apostle Paul, "In Him we live and move and have our being."[4]

Lenny LeBlanc in his song "There Is None Like You" divulges to us such overwhelming feelings of gratitude and tender intimacy that can only be found in a soul in touch with divinity. Straight from his heart he cried out to God saying, "There is none like You." And every other passionate worshipper who has heard the beautiful rendition of this song could not help but join him to cry out to God, "There is none like You!"

No matter what you do, know, or have, the experience of knowing Jesus is second to none. Do you know Him? What do you really know? Are you in a living relationship or a mere religious form? Until you experience worship in spirit and truth you can never understand all of this.

Some are trying to fill the emptiness of their souls with money, power, fame, or position. Others have made traditions, creeds, and all kinds of sacrifice their passion, but nothing in the whole world can really satisfy the hunger of the human soul.

The economists say "Human needs are insatiable...." Not even religion can satisfy the true craving of any soul. The longing of man can only be satisfied by the true source of life.

As we connect to God, the giver and sustainer of our being, we will discover an eternal fountain flowing for the nourishment of our souls. The price has been paid but the choice is yours.

CHAPTER TWO

THE COLD WAR OVER WORSHIP

The deep spiritual need of the human soul all over the world is the same irrespective of race, tongue, and tribe. The hunger in the soul of man in the civilized world is no different from that of a soul among the primitive tribes of the Amazon forest. Worship is an issue of the heart.

The sophistication of a cathedral with a well-planned order of worship does not translate into a soul-stirring worship experience. Worship is not an event; it is an encounter designed to nourish the soul of man as it reconnects to God, who is the true source of abundant life. This is the reason why the enemy of our soul is not bothered by our traditions or creeds. He is happy when we focus on the shadow instead of the substance of worship. He is not troubled when religious leaders get worked up trying to protect the liturgical heritage of their mission. But he trembles at the slightest clue that a group of persons are united in their effort to encounter God. When our obsession and motivation is more about proving the superiority of our liturgical position than in creating the right atmosphere for worship, we are only helping the agenda of the enemy.

The enemy enjoys the passion we display trying to protect our most cherished position to the detriment of true worship. Unfortunately, many religious people are oblivious to the potency of the enemy's strategy in this war over worship. With such religious folks, every idea or opinion must be challenged as long as it originated from a fellow with a different view or orientation.

Surprisingly, this cold war is common among religious leaders because they allow their personal interest and pride to get in the way of the sacred art of worship. Chief among them is the subtle battle between church pastors and their music directors or music ministers. This shameful and unhealthy development is the reason behind the setback we suffer in our worship.

Liturgical Conflicts

The task of preparing qualitative and liturgically appropriate music for worship has never been an easy one for any music director/minister and the choir. The challenge is not so much in the teaching and interpretation of the music, but in the ability to choose a material that is able to meet the need of a particular audience at a particular point in time. An unsatisfactory selection and performance may be tolerated during the regular weekly worship service by some, but this will be one sin too many during special services like the Christmas carol night. In some congregations, as far as they are concerned, this is where both their pride and tradition are at stake. Therefore, until it is done and over, there is no respite for all concerned.

This was the kind of pressure a beloved friend had to deal with as he tried to put in place the finishing touches to the choir's presentation for the 2005 carol night. (He was the music director of a reputable branch of one of the mainstream denominations). This particular rehearsal was not an easy one for him. He was having a tough time harmonizing the singing of the choir with the steps of the choreographers. In the midst of all this he noticed the entrance of the church pastor, acknowledged his presence without any hesitation, and excused himself from the rehearsal to attend to the pastor, who obviously had something to say.

As they exchanged compliments, he observed the stern look on the pastor's face, but before he could discern why, the pastor said, "Is this thing [the choreography] a part of your presentation during the Christmas carol service?"

"Yes sir," the music director answered.

With his suspicions now confirmed, the pastor went on to say, "I'm sorry, I will not permit that here."

Bewildered by what he just heard, the director asked for some form of explanation.

But the pastor firmly declared, "I just don't want it," as he began to walk away.

In an effort to stir up some sympathy, the music director reminded him that the group had been working on this for quite a while now and that it would be so discouraging to trash all their efforts without any serious explanation given. But again the pastor affirmed his stance by saying, "Sorry, my mind is made up." He then turned and walked away.

The music director stood there disoriented and discouraged. He never saw it coming. It was so hard for him to comprehend the whole thing because this was not the first time he was making use of the choreographers as part of his presentation. He had been careful to make sure nothing indecent or misleading was used as a part of their performance, and now he just couldn't figure it out as he stood there wondering what went wrong.

But only a few days later the pieces of the puzzle began to fall into place. News reached him that some very powerful and influential individuals in the church were the ones who talked the pastor into his stand. They were serious adherents to the traditional worship liturgy of this denomination. They were conformists to that which had been handed down from one generation to another—conservative hardliners who could not stand the new and so-called creative ideas championed by the younger generation.

As far as they were concerned, their way of worship should be left just the way it had been and anyone daring enough to get in their way must be ready for a showdown. Amazingly, this group of people can be found in almost every religious group.

Walking into the midst of this sanctimonious group, one can hardly imagine the potency of the arsenal in their possession, but this is better imagined than experienced. Don't take them for granted, because with them it only takes a spark to get their fire going.

A Phenomenon of Coup d'état

For most Africans, coup d'état is a well-known phenomenon. Between 1966 and 1989 there were at least seven successful and failed coups in Nigeria alone. These coups were orchestrated mainly by the military boys, with a few in which some civilians were involved.

During this period, coup d'état was a regular phenomenon in Nigeria. The sound of the country's national anthem or some military music via the radio or TV was the first signal of these coups. This was usually followed by the words "Fellow Nigerians" or "Fellow countrymen." On hearing this, the average Nigerian knew the previous regime had been toppled by another who had just assumed office. If this were not the case then it was the news of a failed coup d'état.   T h e r e was little or nothing anyone could do to the military boys in those days, and so the whole nation looked on in fear and uncertainty.

Sometimes the religious arena can be very intricate, bearing traces of the coup d'état. In a place where everyone appears to be innocent, friendly, and spiritually inclined, it is so difficult to imagine the presence and degree of frenzy on display. The quietude notwithstanding, it may not take that long for you to realize you have walked into a battlefield.

In the political arena, people make their intentions known and employ all kinds of intrigues to outwit the opposition. But

I tell you the truth: the intrigue in the political arena is only a child's play compared with that of the religious arena.

A careful study of human history will convince you that the religious arena has a much more active and fierce war, which has been there for centuries. Part of the reason why it may not have occupied the front pages of the daily news is because it employs the use of impeccable intrigue.

In some cases, several unsuspecting individuals have been craftily manipulated and used as weapons in the cold war to their disadvantage. Their words and actions were carefully orchestrated by some powerful interest group to achieve the selfish purpose of the group.

Due to the high level of subtlety involved, most people are only able to notice it after the deal has been signed and sealed. Unlike most of the coup d'état that are common in Africa, this is a well thought out plan with the tracks well covered.

The use of such intrigue in the religious arena can be startling. Some years ago when I was just a religious boy, it was astounding to accept as true some of the manifestations that followed the religious meetings of my church and some other congregations.

I saw and heard about outbursts of anger among church folks that were not common at the gatherings of non-religious social clubs. Elders were shouting down one another over little difference of opinion.

There were times when such disagreements ended up as a free-for-all fight in which hymnals, small church bells, chairs, and other handy items were used as missiles against those of the opposing camp.

But the most amazing thing of all is that after such dishonorable incidents during the midweek meeting, come Sunday you would see this same congregation gathered together under the same roof singing and dancing. Certainly they did offer prayers to God, and well-prepared sermons were preached, even though it may just be another way to trade punches indirectly. And this was called "worship service." Was it really a worship encounter or the encounter of "war-ships"?

Sometimes it became difficult to tell when people were actually speaking by the unction of the Holy Spirit or by manipulative intent. It was a period in which the various interest groups were fully engaged in one form of campaign or the other in a desperate move to win some key or tough individuals to their agenda, even though their sugarcoated words may just be another ploy to accomplish their selfish agenda.

Before most serious decisions were reached, a meeting of the high and mighty must have been conveyed to conclude on issues before they were brought to the general body. It was at such powerful caucus meetings—usually held in somebody's apartment—that the agenda of called meetings were actually discussed and decided.

This is where they carefully plotted out the moving of the motion and the support that would help them accomplish their particular interest. You don't want to know all the serious details if you really want to remain a true worshipper, so let's leave it at that.

There were times when leaders had to include certain individuals in the officiating of the worship, not necessarily because they had something tangible to offer. It was just another way of making the pendulum swing in favor of the leader. All these maneuvers were done under the cover of worship.

It is sad to note that the sinister strategies of certain individuals are the reasons why most places of worship have become dead and dry. You don't have to look that far; they are everywhere. In some places the hymnal and the church bell may not have been hurled at those of the opposite camp, but there may exist a more subtle and dangerous battle.

There is nothing as deceptive as making someone believe you are with them when in fact you are just waiting for them to fall so you can have your way. They systematically withdraw their support for someone or a course of action when they are most needed simply because of their wicked selfish motives.

Instrumentalists and singers will purposely refuse to give their best during the worship just to score a point or make someone look less proficient. Others will stage a subtle walk-out by finding some excuse to be away when they are most needed. Others will refuse to show up just to demonstrate how important they are. This is the spirit of rebellion that is prominent in coup d'état. Those with this spirit find it hard to celebrate and rejoice over the success of others. They are self-centered, overambitious, overbearing, and always want to be in the limelight. With them no other person can be better, and nothing anybody does is good enough. It is the spirit of coup d'état, rebellion, and witchcraft. It does not seek to glorify the Father; it is the enemy's strategy to reduce worship to mere religious routine and lifeless social activity.

The Stimulus of a Premature Delivery

The use of high-level intrigue in the religious arena is more often than not the reason people misconstrue worship. The presence of this cold war is why some sincere but frustrated leaders or parishioners are forced to quit their place of service in a given mission before their time elapses there. Somehow, somewhere, they got tired of the fighting and scheming which negated their desire for a meaningful and qualitative worship experience.

When they were no longer able to stand the constant combat, they opted for a more peaceful life. They chose to move on by simply slipping out.

More often than not, as these individuals move away, others on whom they have some degree of influence will follow suit. Consequently, this may lead to the breakup of that religious group into two or more rival factions.

When people are forced to move from one congregation to another, they hope to find some succor and real worship somewhere. But the truth is that such premature delivery occasioned by dissatisfaction and bitterness may never be able to create a worship atmosphere free of suspicion and unhealthy criticism. And so the battle continues, even when the opposition is only a figment of our imagination, thereby giving room for the spirit of strife, and we begin to compete against ourselves.

When the reason why we do what we do is to outshine somebody or the other group, the purpose of worship will record another major setback. Wherever suspicion and bitterness exist, it is usually very difficult to have a meaningful worship experience. In this place, sensuality dominates the decisions and judgment of the people, and so it becomes just another religious gathering.

Those who have tasted this bitter and suffocating pill occasioned by the cold war in worship are not so quick to join just another congregation. Whenever they finally make up their minds, they do not want to be neck-deep in the nitty-gritty of religious affairs. They have learnt not to drink from troubled waters. Like the psalmist in Psalm 23, they would rather wait for God to lead them beside the still waters for the restoration of their wounded souls.

An Age-Long Battle

The oldest and longest battle of the human race can be found in the religious circle. The reason for the jealousy and bitterness in the heart of Cain against Abel was worship related. Once Abel and his sacrifice were accepted and Cain's rejected, the battle began (Genesis 4:3-8). The shedding of the righteous blood of many prophets and priests by their own people across the ages stems from this battle too. Once they became a threat to the interests of certain persons, the plot to eliminate them was set in motion (Matthew 23:35).

The tough times Jesus endured all through His earthly pilgrimage and ministry are traceable to this cold war. Most of the fights He had were related to the Sabbath day of worship. The religious leaders in the days of His earthly ministry built so many laws around the Sabbath that it became a problem anytime Jesus showed up on a Sabbath day.

His teachings and miracles made a great impact on a great number of people, thereby making the traditions and leaders of the Jews unpopular. Unable to stand the attention He was getting from the people, they thought it wise to discredit Him using the laws they had built around the Sabbath as their tool.

On one occasion the Pharisees accused His disciples of transgressing the traditions of the elders, and in response to this Jesus told them they were the ones who transgressed the commandment of God by their traditions, thereby making the Word of God of no effect (Matthew 15:1-6).

All these religious leaders cared about was their tradition. If the healing of the sick and the deliverance of the oppressed and afflicted is what got them fuming with anger, then this Sabbath thing must be the hoax of a dead religious form, and this cannot be worship.

Whenever the selfish motive of mortal man is hidden behind the cloak of religion, it is to ensnare those who dare to challenge the powers that be. Anyone bold enough to challenge them must be ready to take a lot of punches below the belt.

Men who seek public attention and recognition are a danger to worship because of their inordinate ambitions, and the sad reality is that many of them are in church leadership. Such leaders enjoy the feeling of being "in charge." You can see it in their appearance, you can feel it in their utterances, and it is evident in their titles. As long as it suits them, all is well, and if it doesn't suit them, there will be trouble. They are the inspiration behind most of the traditions, dogmas, and legalism of man in the religious arena. Such self-centered leaders are quick to accuse those who differ with them about breaking the longstanding tradition and heritage of the body to intimidate and discredit them.

More often than not, the recurring emphasis on the tradition and heritage of the body are used as weapons by which these leaders keep their people under their control to cripple the opposition.

These leaders make others believe they possess an exclusive knowledge about the worship of God which can also be explained by a few who are consecrated and commissioned by them. Therefore, if you have not been recognized by this exalted group, you must be careful handling such sacred and delicate issues which are of great interest to them, or else they will rock your boat.

Ideological and Intellectual Conflicts

It is amazing that the yardstick by which some are considered authorities on the subject of worship is their doctorate degree in theology. By such undue emphasis on the wisdom and knowledge acquired through the teachings of mortal men, some with a doctorate degree in psychology have been empowered with the responsibility of defining acceptable behaviors in worship.

When it comes to spiritual issues like worship, it is foolish to brag about what mortal man has to offer by our academic credentials. In the arena of worship, what you "know" is not a thing of the head, it is an issue of the Spirit.

Some overbearing and zealous people have tried to reduce worship to an academic exercise or some philosophical opinion void of the divine and supernatural life of the Spirit, thereby giving room to fallacy.

When religious form is mistaken for true worship, men like Karl Marx have reason to say "religion is the opium of the people."[1]

Karl Marx had a firsthand experience of religion, having been born into a family with a long lineage of Jewish background, but the story would have been different if only he had encountered a living and loving relationship with Jehovah God instead of a religious form. I believe he would have shared a different message with his generation and others to come if only he had encountered the substance and not the shadow. The influence he left behind, which led to the rise of communism and anti-Semitism in most parts of the world, would have been different.

Worship is not religion. Worship is an overflow of the intimate fellowship from the heart resulting from a relationship with the Almighty, but religion is the arousing of sentiments from our association with certain doctrines and forms. One is a divine love relationship while the other is a fanatical devotion to a school of thought.

The fire that stirs up worship from the heart is like a little flame kindled in the woods during a dry summer day. It may have been very small, but in no time it will burst out into a mighty and powerful inferno consuming everything that comes across its path.

All we need in our worship experience—which is often saturated with dry wood and stubble (mere religion)—is just a little fire. Just a little fire and all around us will in no time burst into flames. When the fire comes, all theories, ideologies, dogmas, and traditions of men will be placed where they truly belong. At such moments, the best of mortals will be too frail to stand the touch of the immortal and invisible God. When the prophet Isaiah encountered the divine presence of the Almighty, his flesh could not stand it. Many who claim to be religious have not come to know what it really means to worship.

Denominational Prejudice

In the first century, the conflicting opinions and teachings of the Sadducees, the Pharisees, the Hellenistic Jews, and the Gnostics made worship one complicated and difficult affair for people. Not much has changed in our world today; the doctrinal differences between the orthodox, the evangelicals, the Pentecostals, and other self-proclaimed authorities in the religious arena have introduced a far more complex problem that has become a bane to worship.

In the history of the church, no other single factor can be more responsible for the conflicts within her walls than that caused by our different positions about worship.

Denominational walls, segregation, and prejudice exist in the body of Christ as a result of this. The battle for the superiority of one liturgical form over another or one form of music against another has always been a problem.

There has been too much emphasis on our difference, the superiority of one doctrine or creed above that of others. In so doing, we promote our weaknesses above our strengths and those things which tear us apart over those things which unite us.

The determination of some to enforce their most cherished positions has done more harm than good. The sad truth is that we have failed to realize that not one of us has the capacity to make any man truly worship. We lack the capacity and ability to make our own heart or that of any other burn with the fire that is from above. Only the Lord Jesus can baptize with the Holy Spirit and fire (Luke 3:16). When the Spirit and fire come upon a man, it has the capacity to transform him into a worshipper. Then you will not need to enforce anything—worship will become a natural response.

If we are continually trying to force worship, this is an indication that we ourselves lack the fire which stirs the soul to worship. If it is really there, then you don't have to impose it. This is the Lord's business.

You can hide a needle in a sack of hay but not a matchstick with the smallest flame; it will consume the whole thing. Kurt Kaiser in the hymn "Pass It On" shed some light on this by setting the following words to music: It only takes a spark to get a fire going, And soon all those around can warm up in its glowing; That's how it is with God's love, Once you've experienced it; You spread His love to everyone You want to pass it on.[2]

CHAPTER THREE

WHERE ON EARTH IS THE WORSHIPPING CHURCH?

W eek in and out, people wander from one religious house to the other to engage in what they call worship, yet some observers find it increasingly difficult to tell the essence of it all. There seems to be little or no difference between these gatherings and some secular functions, except for the form of godliness and sanctimonious appearance of the religious folks.

Sometimes the emphasis has been more on the passion of the community for her form of worship than for God, who is the reason for the community, thereby making it difficult to tell the difference between what is called worship and entertainment, as can be found in any other gathering where people are passionate for a common cause.

When our worship is more of a performance art than an encounter with divinity, it leaves people wondering about the relevance of a religious community. Furthermore, the lifestyles of worship leaders and other key players that are not compatible with the teachings of the Holy Book make the whole thing look like a joke. That notwithstanding, the inherent thirst in the soul of man to reconnect to the true source of life is enough to stir in man a determination to keep searching until it encounters true worship. And so the battle continues.

It's a Contagious Influence

A worship leader burning for more of God with genuine passion will not have to cajole people to get them to worship passionately. Once they are able to see and feel the genuine passion of the worship leader, they will become willing to have a taste of what he or she possesses.

A.W. Tozer once said, "Worship means 'to feel in the heart.' A person who merely goes through the form and does not feel anything is not worshipping. Worship also means to 'express in some appropriate manner'...."[1]

Without a sincere emotional connection, it will become a fruitless struggle to encounter true worship. If we must worship in spirit and in truth, then we must be able to feel in our hearts some of the prompting of the Spirit stirring us to respond to the Father's call.

Worship leaders who come in feeling God in their hearts are far ahead of those who come in to lead by their religious sentiments or fleshly abilities. Those who come in feeling God in their heart are conscious of the availability of the divine power to stir up others in worship. Those feeding from such ministrations can testify that the true longing of their souls has been ministered to.

Whenever people's expectations are surpassed by what they have encountered, they are more likely to return to worship again and again. When a leader is truly intimate with the Lord, the presence of God upon his life and ministry will soon become visible to all. This leader's attitude toward worship is not the "I already know it all" attitude. His hunger for the manifest presence shows his total dependence on God. His training, knowledge, and other abilities notwithstanding, he has learnt to trust God to give the leading for each worship experience and knows he must surrender all to bring God glory.

A.W. Tozer also said that worship "...is not a feeling only. It is an attitude and a state of mind. It is a sustained act, subject to varying degree of intensity and perfection."[2] For a worship leader to be both effective and efficient he or she needs to strike a balance between worshipping with their skills and their spiritual sensitivity. Something very important seems to be missing in most worship experiences because we fail to allow the Lord to show us what we must do; and so our entire sacrifice and effort end up in futility. Worship is more than what any man can cook up. Tozer puts it this way: "That which I can explain will never bring me to a place of awe. It can never fill me with astonishment or wonder or admiration."[3]

Without the help of the Lord, we will not be able to bring people to the place of worship. If you are bent on a particular tradition, style, form, method, or doctrine, you will do more harm than good. You may enjoy the kudos of men and miss the purpose of heaven.   Those who burn with a fresh passion to worship have been brought to a place of awe. They live in continuous awe of the Lord, and they know the importance of the manifest presence and ministry of the Holy Spirit in worship. It is from this place of intimate fellowship with the Spirit that their hearts burn with the true flame of worship.When your heart is burning with a strong hunger for God, you look forward to fellowship with the Lord like one who is looking forward to meeting with an intimate friend you have not seen for a while.

To look forward to such reunion does cause some excitement and anticipation, and when the moment finally arrives you want to make the most of it by keeping away every distraction. This is common with those in a love relationship but is so hard to come by among religious people.

This Generation

Worship from one generation to another is always influenced by the trend and development of that generation. There were eras in which intellectualism was celebrated over spirituality all around the world, and it did influence the worship of the church. Such was the period in which the worship and doctrine of the church was watered down to the ideology and philosophy of mortal man. This happened to be the major challenge of the church in the Renaissance era. A careful study of the Renaissance era reveals that "this period in time marked the rebirth of humanism and the revival of cultural achievements for their own sake in all forms of art including music."[4]

The church of the Renaissance era had not fully recovered from the setback of the Middle Ages period before this boisterous wind touched down. "The Renaissance began in times of religious turmoil. The late Middle Ages saw a period of political intrigue surrounding the Papacy, culminating in the Western Schism, in which three men simultaneously claimed to be true Bishop of Rome."[5] In this period, tradition and human philosophy triumphed over spirituality in the worship life of the church.

In our generation, the problem is much more complex. The things which were once an abomination and scarcely spoken of in public have become a norm in society.

This generation has too many things standing in the way of true worship. In addition to the inherited problems of previous generations we have our own peculiar troubles to deal with. But still there are those who have made up their minds to go all out for God.

Wherever hungry souls are able to encounter the sweet presence of the Lord, it should not be a problem for them to settle down to worship. Like Peter, they would not mind building their tabernacle there (Luke 9:33). Moments like this can be overwhelming and life-transforming. Those who limit worship to a thing of the head or the enforcing of certain traditions and denominational position are fighting a lost battle.

Years back, there were churches in Europe and America that were more concerned about their traditions and doctrines, but today you can find only a few old folks there. They worship in an altar that has no fire to keep their souls spiritually warm. The younger generation has moved on.

Sometimes we try to make people worship our method of worship, and then we wonder why the pews are not fully occupied. Our worship form does not have the power to satisfy the deep longing of hungry souls. God is the only true longing and satisfaction of any soul.

Many churches have become mere city monuments, while others have been converted to mosques or temples of one of the Eastern religions because their tradition and religion were not strong enough to keep the desperate souls of their parishioners. When we spend valuable time defending our positions, we end up losing the invaluable time needed to adequately prepare for a qualitative time of worship.

You can't wade through muddy water and hope to show up on the other side pleasant in the sight of men. We must learn to focus on the things that will profit the kingdom as we give our heart to promoting worship in spirit and in truth.

It is wrong for us to act as if we are the reservoir of God's position on every issue. The all-wise and all-knowing God is too much for mortals to figure out. God reveals Himself and we are given the grace to know Him, and the best of this knowledge is only in part.

When we are recognized among men as learned or as an authority in certain fields of study, we must be careful not to act as if we have been given the right to validate the worship others offer to God, for worship is in spirit and only He who sees and knows the true content of our spirit has the right to validate the worship that is offered to Him.

Tozer said, "In some circles God has been abridged, reduced, modified, edited, changed, and amended until He is no longer the God whom Isaiah saw, high and lifted up."[6]

The God that Isaiah saw is beyond the comprehension of man; He is high and lifted up above the intellect of man.

Except the Lord grants us the grace, we are not qualified to talk on sensitive subjects like worship. But when we do, we must recognize that the Holy Spirit is the only authority on this subject.

Except the Lord reveals to us, the very best of our effort will amount to making a mockery of ourselves. Our finite wisdom, knowledge, and understanding are grossly inadequate when it comes to the subject of worship. What we know is limited to certain areas and experiences that are often influenced by circumstances and situations at some particular point in time. There is much more than we can imagine. Worship is beyond our imagination. For us to bring people to a place of worship we must go beyond our mental abilities. Worship is in the spirit.

Identifying the True and Sincere Passion of the Soul

Until a man is able to identify what he really needs, he is a confused and purposeless being. In the process of trying to identify the true desire of our hearts, it will become necessary for us to sincerely seek the answers to certain questions which will help narrow our scope and help us encounter true worship.

For thousands of years mankind struggled to provide the correct answers to the questions of worship until Jesus came to lead us out of the woods. While talking with the Samaritan woman at Jacob's well, He knew that would be the spot where the all important issue of the entire human race would be addressed.

In this time of Jesus' earthly ministry, Jews had nothing to do with Samaritans due to the prolonged differences between them, and to add to it all, this was even a woman. But Jesus asked her for a drink of water. As expected, her response was like "how dare you?" and Jesus got her right where He wanted her. It was the opportunity for Him to address the issue of tradition and religion that has kept many away from true worship.

He began to make her realize the true thirst of her life and then went on to tell her He actually came to quench that thirst. She could not see how Jesus would do this because her natural mind was still in control, and she wondered how He would be able to get the water from Jacob's well.

She did not understand that Jesus was speaking of the yearning of her soul. She even thought Jesus meant "there is this water from a Jewish well that is far better than that from Jacob's well," so she began to defend her much cherished tradition by trying to prove the superiority of the water source.

She traced the tradition of her religion down to the patriarch Jacob and his children, who became the twelve tribes of Israel, to defend her stand. You know, this is exactly what many of us are doing today. It is the only reason some worship where they worship, when they worship, and how they worship.

They will tell you that their denomination or tradition was started by one well-known religious man who was greatly used by God some years ago. Whether God is doing something new is none of their business. As far as they are concerned, nothing can be greater or better. But you know, Jesus said something which opened the eyes of this woman. He said, "Everyone who drinks this water will be thirsty again, but whoever drinks the water I give him will never thirst. Indeed the water I give him will become a spring of water welling up to eternal life."[7]

When she heard this, she could not wait to drink this water that would quench her thirst once and for all. For the first time she heard of something better than what her tradition had to offer. Though it was difficult to accept, the sound of it held so much promise that it was too good to ignore. She saw for the first time in her life an opportunity to satisfy the true hunger of her soul, so she concluded in her heart to give it a try. Now she could no longer hold back and suddenly cried out, "...give me this water...."   This was not the effort of man, it was the Lord revealing to this woman the shallowness and emptiness of what she had been holding onto for so long. What are you holding onto? Is it worth all the trouble? Can there be more than what you have? If what you have does not satisfy, if after the whole experience you still feel this emptiness or frustration, if at the end it leaves you with a deeper longing for that which was elusive throughout the whole experience, then you are far from the true source which gives fresh passion to worship.

The water that the Lord gives does not only satisfy, it quenches your thirst and ends the desperate search of your soul. Those who have tasted the real thing have no desire for something else.

Jesus said this water will become a spring welling up to eternal life. He will deposit in you an incessant supply that is more than enough. If you come close enough you will see the difference and it will stir in you a desire to have it.

This particular discussion between Jesus and the Samaritan woman provokes questions that, when well attended to, should help us find the worshipping church. Some of these questions include the following:

1. Is This Worship Outside the Box?

Too often, what we call worship is a straitjacket experience that makes men more religious than intimate with God. As Jesus continued His conversation with this woman, she realized that she was not talking to an ordinary man. So she said, "You must be a prophet." This was when she began to search for answers to some of the questions about worship that had been troubling her for a long time. She said, "Our fathers worshiped on this mountain, but you Jews claim that the place where we must worship is in Jerusalem."[9]

She wanted an answer to an issue that was a serious problem in her time and still is today. Back then both the Jews and the Samaritans believed that worship is an issue of geographical location or the sacredness of a place, but today it is worse. There are people from a particular church or denomination who discriminate against those who are not part of them. They boastfully speak of their group to imply that real worship is limited to their own denomination or church, but they are very wrong.

The Lord is too sovereign and eternal to be held within the four walls of a church or denomination. Just when you think you have it all figured out, God will show up in some other places least expected. You may succeed in limiting your worship within the box you have created, but you cannot keep God within that box.

The Azusa Street Revival in the United States over a century ago is one good example. In those days, the mainstream churches thought God was limited to their philosophy, traditions, doctrines, big titles, and cathedrals. But this was when God began to stir the hearts of people for something more. People suddenly got fed up with all these things, and they became hungry for something more. This longing led them to the Azusa Street Mission.

Once there, they became free from religious forms and were able to pursue their passion. In this meeting they all had one thing in common: a strong hunger for an encounter with God.

As they continued, their passion became strong enough to attract the presence and power of the Lord to the Azusa mission. Great and awesome things began to happen as the Lord rewarded their hunger with many unusual manifestations.

The news of this great revival soon spread far and wide, and people started coming from every part of America and beyond to Azusa. They abandoned magnificent church buildings and well organized liturgical settings with reputable religious leaders for the common but Spirit-filled worship at the Azusa mission.

But then we must remember you can't box God. "It is generally acknowledged that Pentecostalism began with the Azusa street revival in Los Angeles, in 1906...for half a century the Holy Spirit movement was largely confined to the Pentecostal group of churches."[10] But after approving of this gathering with wonderful displays of His awesome presence and glory at the Azusa mission, God again proved to be sovereign when He turned away from the Azusa mission and the heart of the people went with Him. Why would God do that? Again, God will not allow worship to be put in a straitjacket.

Roberts Liardon in his book *God's Generals* said, "The destruction of Azusa mission was the writing Apostolic Faith across the top of the building."[11] When this happened, "people began to suspect it was becoming another denomination. There was division and it was no longer a free spirit for all as it had been."[12] And Liardon added, "The work had become one more revival party and body."[13]

When we try to lay claim to what is only possible by the hand of God, He will walk away leaving us empty and frustrated.

In some places, all they have left of the mighty move of God is only a signpost or some monument. It has become a "once upon a time" story. If we will stay on with God, we will see His glory as of old. Our God is the same yesterday, today, and forever (Hebrews 13:8). God is God all by Himself, and His glory He will not give to any other.

2. What Is the Priority in This Worship?

Our short stay on this side of eternity is full of challenges and a constant pressure to rise to a place of relevance and achievements. In this race against time, many in their anxiety have lost consciousness of the need to set their priorities right, and it is sad to see this water down our worship experience.

There is always a divine strategy for us to make the most of every opportunity and resources within our reach. It is only when we are conscious of this that we are able to bring all the glory to God with every worship experience.

In the encounter between Jesus and the Samaritan woman by Jacob's well, this divine strategy was at play. From the very beginning Jesus had His priority set. The woman was ready to win an argument, but He was out to make one more worshipper. When she argued about the right location for worship He made her see that worship is in the realm of spirit and truth. He did not convert her to Judaism; rather He showed her how to satisfy the longing of the Father. He said to her, "... the time is coming and is already here when true worshipers will worship the Father in spirit and in truth. The Father is looking for anyone who will worship him that way. For God is Spirit, so those who worship him must worship in spirit and in truth."[14]

When He focused her heart on the real thing, the true needs of her soul were met. When we reduce worship to our traditions, intellectual views, feelings, and emotions we give people dead religion. Trying to make man access God's presence by any other means will end in frustration. When our worship is focused on increasing our membership rather than building worshippers, we should not be surprised to see the ugly manifestations of the flesh in our meetings.

Romans 8:8 says, "So then they that are in the flesh cannot please God." We can only gain access to God by "...comparing spiritual things with spiritual."[15] It is an established truth that "the natural man receiveth not the things of the Spirit of God for they are foolishness unto him: neither can he know them, because they are spiritually discerned."[16]

Many of us like that Samaritan woman limit the worship of God to a place, style, or form of worship, and this is a waste of time. The best of our human intellect, church, or denomination is not good enough to make anybody worship in spirit and in truth. This is why Jesus once said to the religious leaders, "Woe to you teachers of the law and Pharisees, you hypocrites! You travel over land and sea to win a single convert, and when he becomes one, you make him twice as much a son of hell as you are."[17]

If what we call soul winning or evangelism is just to make someone a member of our church or organization, we have failed. Unless that soul is so transformed into a worshipper that the watching world sees the glory of the Lord through him/her, then all our efforts were in vain.

3. What Is the Goal of Our Effort?

Yes, God may bless our effort to build something in His name, but He will have no problem walking away from it when it becomes the reason for us being cold and passive in our worship. The Lord is more interested in us building lives than in building world renown.

At the dedication of Solomon's temple, the glory of the Lord fell so mightily that the priests could not minister. Many want us to believe that the glory fell because of the magnificent structure of the temple, but a careful study of the Scripture reveals that the glory fell as God's own response to the worship offered Him, not in response to the magnificent building.

When we are truly worshipping in spirit, the glory will fall. Sometimes when this happens it has nothing to do with our method of worship. This is not because we have carefully followed a planned program; it may well be the opposite. When our worship always goes as planned, chances are that we are too much in-charge and there is no room for the Holy Spirit to spice it up.

Through a careful study of the Scriptures you will see that though God blessed the effort of His people to build a magnificent permanent place of worship, it was never required of man. The idea and vision had always been the dream and passion of one of God's servants, such as David.

God's view of man's desire to build Him a permanent house can be seen in His response to David's intention through the prophet Nathan. He said,

> Go and tell David my servant, Thus says the Lord, "You shall not build a house for me to dwell in; for I have not dwelt in a house since the day I brought up Israel to this day, but I have gone from tent to tent and from one dwelling place to another. In all places where I have walked with all Israel, have I spoken a word with any of the judges of Israel, whom I commanded to shepherd my people, saying, 'Why have you not built for me a house of cedar?' Now therefore, thus shall you say to My servant David, Thus says the LORD of host, 'I took you from the pasture, from following the sheep, to be leader over My people Israel....'"[18]

The Lord's desire is far above a need for a house of cedar. He does not desire us to spend all our resources and time on a building project at the expense of our fellowship with Him. The only time He chided His people over a physical place of worship, it was because they were indifferent and passive about the place of meeting, which was in ruins, yet they had built for

49

themselves cozy houses (Haggai 1:2-5). It was a problem of selfishness and misplaced priority. It is a great privilege and honor to be counted worthy to build a meeting place for worship to the glory of God, but it is an error to make it our major focus. If the Lord lays it on our hearts to build, it will not cost us so much trouble to accomplish this assignment.

So many church leaders who were commissioned of God to build souls for the kingdom have become more passionate about building structures, organizations, and denominations than in shepherding the flocks. They have become so obsessed with this passion that little or no time is left to focus on building God's people. This is the reason why some places of worship suffer stagnation. You want to know why? God walked away from them.

After the dedication of Solomon's temple, the Lord appeared to Solomon that night in response to the prayer and sacrifice he offered during the dedication of the temple. The Lord said to him, "I have heard your prayer and have chosen this place to myself for an house of sacrifice."[19]

God accepted it as a house of sacrifice (an act of worship), but He also made it clear that He would cast out this temple from His sight if the people turned from His ways (2 Chronicles 7:19-22). In the days of the prophet Jeremiah, the Lord became angry with the rebellious house of Israel and said,

> While you were doing all these things, declares the LORD, I spoke to you again and again, but you did not listen; I called you, but you did not answer. Therefore, what I did to Shiloh I will now do to the house that bears my Name, the temple you trust in, the place I gave to you and your fathers. I will thrust you from my presence, just as I did all your brothers, the people of Ephraim.[20]

When the Lord made good His promise and the temple was destroyed by their enemies, it did not make God homeless because it was only a place of sacrifice, not His permanent address (2 Chronicles 7:12,15). By idolizing the temple the people departed from the divine purpose and attracted divine judgment.

Churches and Christian organizations all over the world are motivated by a variety of mission statements and visions, but if they fail to produce worshippers, heaven will give the resources of the kingdom to others who are ready to bring God glory.

4. What Is the Pursuit of This Mission?

In the year 2005, the Lord gave me an unusual and frightening experience in a vision of the night. All of a sudden, I saw the heavens open and a terrifying creature of metallic form like a man came out. It must have been over 450 feet tall. As I watched, it picked up one of the magnificent mega-church buildings I am familiar with in Nigeria and dashed it to the ground to destroy it. As it did, people were gripped with fear and ran away to a safe distance.

Immediately after this, I was taken to an open field in a twilight setting that was gradually being overshadowed with darkness. There were people all over this field, and I saw that some of them were suddenly being transformed into a glorious appearance which caused them to glow with a brilliant light. Instantly I was carried into what looked like an uncompleted building on one end of the field, and I saw a well-known minister of the gospel ministering to people. As he laid his hands on them their faces became radiant with light, and as this happened he sent them away urging them with a passionate cry, "Go, go, go...!" As he did, they soon became a great crowd covering the face of the earth.

Just then I gained consciousness, but I could not understand the whole vision. I knew this was a serious message from the Lord so I spent some time asking God to grant me understanding. Sometime later, He opened my understanding to explain the night vision. The Lord told me He is not happy with ministers who are more passionate to build wonderful structures and other things to project themselves at the expense of spending time and kingdom resources to equip the saints for the work of the ministry. They have departed from the reason He gave them to the church as a gift (Ephesians 4:10-16), and therefore their efforts will be in vain.

I was also made to understand that the world is covered with darkness (Isaiah 60:2a), but the Lord expects His people to arise and shine forth to transform the world with the glorious light He blessed us with (gifts and ministries) till the earth is full of His knowledge and glory (Isaiah 60:1,2b,3).

We are living in a time when we will see some mega-structures abandoned by God because they are far from bringing Him glory. They may still be filled with people but the glory of God will be missing.

The Lord will cause people to leave some of these churches, and sometimes they will leave in droves. Why will this happen? The hunger in the heart of these worshippers will exceed that which they are being fed with, and in their determination to encounter God they will relocate.

Don't get me wrong. I am not condemning those who are building mega-structures. If they are following the heartbeat of the Lord for souls and not the pride of the flesh, it will become obvious to all and God will bless it.

When we invest the best of our time, resources, and passions on people, the kingdom of God is promoted on earth and heaven rejoices, but to do contrary is a waste.

Our time here on earth is limited and must be spent wisely. Heaven values our effort to build worshippers over our effort to build a place of worship. This is the reason why God is now blessing and empowering those who are passionate to raise true worshippers all over the world.

Worship is eternal but a building is temporal. The building will fade away but worship will continue for all eternity. I am yet to find a scripture in the New Testament where the emphasis is on the building of a place of worship. In the book of Acts, the apostle Paul puts it this way, "The God who made the world and everything in it is the Lord of heaven and earth and does not live in temples built by hands."[21] But you will find several scriptures where the Lord passionately urged leaders to build up the saints.

After the resurrection, Jesus saw the need to ensure that all His efforts were not in vain so He appeared to some of His disciples. Focusing on Peter, He began to provoke in him a fresh passion to help nurture the sheep. This He reiterated with these words: "Feed my lambs...take care of my sheep.... Feed my sheep."[22]

There is more eternal value in investing in souls than in any building project. On a certain day, the disciples of Jesus called His attention to the beauty of the temple as they admired the majestic masterpiece. They wanted some affirmation from the Lord, but He said to them, "Do you see all these great buildings? Not one stone will be left on another. Every one will be thrown down."[23]

No matter how wonderful our projects are, the only thing of eternal value is the glorious impartation we make upon souls. In the writings of Paul we are made to understand that leaders are nothing but co-laborers with God, working to build God's people, which are the real building (1 Corinthians 3:5-9) . This was confirmed by the apostle Peter in 1 Peter 2:5. The very foundation of this building is Christ Jesus, and this is the foundation we must build upon (1 Corinthians 3:10-15). Some of the church buildings in which John Wesley, Charles Finny, and other great preachers ministered have been converted to mere monuments, but the souls they helped to transform for the kingdom are now the true trophies of their labor in heaven. We must direct our labor to that which is of eternal value and by so doing store up treasures in heaven.

A Church Tragedy

I once heard of a pastor who died in the church leaders' meeting after receiving news that the bank was coming to take over the uncompleted church building. They could not

pay the debt they incurred in their attempt to build an edifice. This pastor on hearing the news died of a broken heart
over a building project. It would have been better if he had
died laboring to transform lives for the kingdom of God. If you
ignore the brokenhearted you will die of a broken heart. There
are those who smile as they pass away and there are others
who are full of regrets as they exit this life. But the truth is that
our everyday actions and decisions will either put a smile on
our face or cover us with shame as we exit this realm.

Buildings and other institutions or organizations may win
us the accolades of this world, but a soul made to worship the
Father in spirit and in truth is the admiration of the angels in
heaven and an asset to God on earth.

Joining the Rat Race

The hidden motive of some churches and ministries to
excel is a passion to build their own little empire. They want
to be recognized as a force to be reckoned with among others,
and so they embark on the project or program. This is the
same spirit that motivated King Jeroboam to walk in error as
revealed in his words: "...If these people go up to offer sacrifice at the temple of the Lord in Jerusalem, they will again give
their allegiance to their lord, Rehoboam king of Judah....On the
fifteenth day of the eighth month, a month of his own choosing,
he offered sacrifices on the altar he had built at Bethel. So he
instituted the festival for the Israelites and went up to the altar
to make offerings. "[24]

The spread of some denominations is just to out-do some
other denomination in the name of church growth or evangelism. It is just to register their presence in certain places to
enlarge their domain. In a place like this, spiritual impact can
be considered accidental because it was not the main purpose
or vision for setting up this church. It is obvious that such religious activities are born out of a sense of insecurity and selfish
motive. They are ill-conceived and often led by those lacking
the call and divine grace of God (1 Kings 12:31). They go on to
put in place stringent measures to make it almost impossible

for their gifted and talented leaders and members to accept invitations to be a blessing to God's people of other denominations, using submission to authority as their guise.

Churches are now organizing programs to make it impossible for their members to go somewhere else, even when it is obvious that such programs have nothing tangible to offer (see 1 Kings 12:32-33 and note the words "device of his own heart"). Sometimes these activities are hurriedly put together just because the church next door announced theirs. They are even scheduled for the same date and time, revealing the spirit of strife and competition as the obvious source of their inspiration.

A good number of those raised under such circumstances are often more religious than regenerated, more denominational-minded than kingdom-minded. Nurtured in an atmosphere of strife, they are more ready to defend their denomination than their faith, for this is the true passion of their souls.

They usually know little or nothing about an intimate and personal relationship with the Father because this is not the reason behind their mission. The sad reality is that they are often far from worshipping in spirit and in truth and they are at best denominational enthusiasts.

Some places of worship only exist in name. Nothing is going on there that is true worship. By the name of their denomination they may have a reputation for being alive, but in the rating of heaven they are dead (Revelation 3:1).

When we build just to make a name for ourselves we are in trouble. This should remind you of something—the building of the tower of Babel. They wanted to make a name for themselves. And the Lord responded to this by confusing their language to frustrate them, and that was the end of the great project (Genesis 11).

What Are We Building Here?

Sometimes people try to hide their selfish motives by claiming they are building for God. But sincerely speaking, can we really build a house for God? He whose dwelling is the unspeakable glory of heaven has said that the earth is at best His footstool. But it is a wonder to know that this same God has chosen to dwell in us, though it is actually us dwelling in Him. Although not all men are acceptable to Him, He has chosen to make him that is humble and contrite in spirit—the one who trembles at His word—the temple of His Spirit (Isaiah 66:1-3).

Any soul redeemed by the blood of the Lamb is a sanctuary made for the presence of the Lord, and this is a greater edifice before God.

When a soul is willing to worship the Father with the deepest longing of the heart, all the resources of heaven will be made available to him.   Jesus, on the last day of the feast at Jerusalem, revealed the passion of heaven when He cried out, "If anyone is thirsty, let him come to me and drink. Whoever believes in me, as the scripture has said, Streams of living water will flow from within him."[25]

This was the last day of the feast of tabernacles. This feast was meant to be a constant reminder of God's abiding presence with His people, but in this particular feast, as in many others, the presence of the Lord was nowhere to be found in their celebration. It was all dry and empty religion without life. There was singing, clapping, dancing, and sermons, just like what happens in many conferences, conventions, revivals, and camp meetings. But it was all empty noise and emotions, empty wind and clouds that lacked the water to refresh the soul of man.

The Lord could take it no more. He cried out with a loud voice, calling to as many as were tired of this dead religious ceremony to come encounter the real thing: "If anyone can identify the true longing of his soul and is thirsty enough to drink from the river of God, out of him will flow a stream of living water!" (John 7:37).

When people return from a meeting where they met with the Lord, they are full of life and joy. It is common to hear them singing and testifying to God's goodness for several days because it has become a stream of joy flowing from their belly.

Don Harris in his song "Such Joy" called it:

Such joy! Such unspeakable joy,
Such peace, an everlasting peace.
Such love, a pure and holy love...[26]

You are His tabernacle. You no longer have to experience a dry and dead religious feast. You can have a continuous feast as you fellowship with the Lord, for the Lord is now in you and you are in Him. Hallelujah!

When this is in you, wherever you show up the glory of the Lord will be revealed. Darkness is turned to light and the dead are quickened to life. From then on all you really long for is the life in the Spirit.   Some years back, as I reflected on the reality of life in the Spirit, a lovely song flowed out of my spirit which I titled "Your Life." This is the passion of my heart expressed in these words of worship:

Your life Lord, (2x) Your life is all I need. Let it be You, no longer me. Your life Lord, (2x) Your life is all I need no longer mine. From the rising of the sun to the going down of the same, Let Your glory fill my temple, Let Your power rule my life.

(Back to the chorus)[27]

Those who have become partakers of the life in the Spirit will tell you that there is nothing like it. When this takes over the life of a city, denominational walls will be broken. Then the Pentecostal will be able to worship in a Baptist church and find a river of the presence of the Lord, and they will not be in a hurry to leave. An Anglican will minister in a Pentecostal setting and people will ask, "Did you say he is an Anglican?"

Who cares if the worship is with classical or contemporary gospel music! If it can truly make God's people worship in spirit and in truth, then to God be the glory. Whatever will cause the heart to burn with a fresh passion to worship God is good for the soul and must be highly sought after.

Is There Room for Others in This Worship?

It is our natural tendency to applaud and associate with that which appeals to us and to criticize and fight against that which does not. Upon this premise I wish to share with you a brief narrative based on a popular Bible story.

It is the twilight of the day as the red sun fades away over the horizon of the dusty open field. The day's job is over and you can see slaves and their masters making their way back home. It has been a long and stressful task of trying to meet the set goal for most of them, and now that the season is almost over there seems to be little or nothing anyone can do to change the course of things. In this homeward journey there appears something unusual. In this caravan of farmers, shepherds, and merchants is found a camel carrying a middle-aged man not cheaply clothed with a robust and healthy appearance, but he wears no happy looks. Much of the journey has been unusually quiet and uneventful.

With him is a young slave in his early thirties named Ziba who has been walking on foot beside him all the way. He observes the look of dissatisfaction written on his master's face and knows this will in some way affect him. He therefore thinks of a way to get his master out of this mood. After taking some deep breaths he finds the courage to break this uneasy calm.

"My master," he says, "I am sure by the end of next season your farm will have exceeded that of our great king." But his master in a cold but ruthless tone says, "It would have been much better if only my father had not granted the request of my overbearing and lazy brother," revealing the bitterness of his soul.

Hoping to focus his attention on the bright side of life, Ziba says, "But, my master, I must salute your courage to have been able to restore the fortune of your father as before within a short time." The sound of this strokes a sensitive chord of his master's ego, but he simply replies "thanks" for the compliment, as if it were some herculean task. "If only that scoundrel had not gone away with half the estate, things would be better off."

Satisfied that he has finally broken the silence, Ziba continues, "My master, pardon me, it is just that I am not as fortunate as you are. At least your brother left you with something to work on, but in my case it was my own father who used my life to secure a loan to sustain his gambling and drinking habits. And when he could not pay his debts I became a slave. Twice was I sold by my masters until I became your slave." His master looks at him with some pity and admiration, and right there Ziba knows he has succeeded in weeping up some compassion from him. This is good because they are now but a few yards from their residence.

"Ziba, I am glad to have you, and it is by your hard work that you have won my favor. In no time your hard work should be able to buy back your freedom and you will become a free man again."

With his face lighting up, Ziba responds, "Without doubt, my greatest joy will come the day I am able to pay for my freedom." But with a vindictive tone his master retorts, "Ziba, I wish my brother was your father's son and the one in your stead." Just then he pauses and gazes off in the distance in amazement.

"Is anything the matter, my master?" Ziba asks.

"I can see a great crowd at my father's house; I hope all is well." After a critical gaze Ziba replies, "My master, this must be some sort of celebration." The suggestion makes some sense and the master replies, "I think you are right, for I can hear the sound of joyful celebration with music, but I am certain my father did not tell me of this celebration." As he climbs down the camel he says with some sense of pride, "Could this be a surprise party for me?"

Just then one of the servants from the house who saw them approaching comes running with excitement, and before they can ask him what is the reason for the celebration he exclaims in one breath, "My master, your younger brother has returned home, and your father has killed the fattened calf and given him his best robe, a ring, and sandals for his feet because he came back alive though looking impoverished and close to death."

Before Ziba can intervene his master is already in a rage, and with clenched fist he kicks the dusty ground to register his displeasure. "I cannot believe this! You mean that scoundrel is the reason for all this noise and wastage? I will have nothing to do with this." And he walks away into the dark, dusty field fuming.

Some of us will be very quick to judge the obnoxious temperament of Ziba's master, who is a type of the elder brother in the prodigal son parable, but unfortunately this happens to be the posture of some self-righteous and legalistic religious people today. Many are so angry with their heavenly Father for blessing the worship of others with His gifts and manifest presence.

Like the elder brother in this story, they are so full of themselves and their achievements. They glory in their self-righteousness and are quick to criticize and condemn others upon whom the grace of God is lavished.

Like the elder brother, they don't want anything to do with such places of worship, and if they could have their way they would close it down. This is carnality and wickedness. They have forgotten that our God is sovereign and does not need our approval to be gracious. We must also remember that He alone knows His divine plan and purpose and which vessel is most appropriate for a particular assignment. One man's meat they say is another man's poison. When we refuse to see the overall kingdom purpose of anything, we deny ourselves the benefits and beauty it adds to the kingdom of God. To come into worship with your preconceived notions and sentiments is a deliberate attempt to frustrate and ruin that worship.

A flower is beautiful all by itself but a bouquet is a greater beauty to behold because it is a combination of various shapes, sizes, colors, and scents.

Life will be too boring if everyone is just like you. Sometimes the reason why we feel lonely and bored is because we have had too much of ourselves. We need to take a stroll outside our little corner to see or listen to someone else, and, I tell you, it will make a lot of difference even when you do not share the same opinion. Being narrow-minded will cut short your joy and benefits in God's kingdom. To worship with fresh passion is to come into worship like a child looking forward to Christmas with excitement and expectancy. In this atmosphere, anything wonderful can happen because right here anything is possible.

The Glory of Unity

During our 2007 worship conference, a friend of mine, Rev. Kunle Oyeniyi, said something in his seminar presentation that caught my attention. He said, "Leaders must understand that in a public worship experience, there cannot be uniformity in expression and responses to worship, but there can be unity."[28]

In a particular worship experience that is in spirit and truth, Mr. A may be moved to respond to the presence of God by weeping while Mr. B is at the same time full of joy and laughter. Most people who try to respond in uniformity are men pleasers. They are those who wear one mask in church and another at home. They are double-faced.

Many who worship in uniformity do so to please certain individuals, and this is often to please leaders who are hard-liners about their method, style, and procedure in worship. They are leaders who are often domineering in nature and enjoy the feeling of being in charge. Some even have it carved into their title to intimidate others: The Minister in Charge. Choosing to differ with them is to present oneself as a rebel and a threat; therefore, some would rather comply with their demands than be real and face their wrath.

But some leaders are sensitive enough to identify the various gifts in the body and are willing to bring them together for the benefit of all. When this is done, an unusual manifestation of God's presence will be experienced by all, thereby stirring a fresh passion to worship. The psalmist puts it this way:

"Behold how good and how pleasant it is for brothers to dwell together in unity!"[29]

That which is celebrated here in this passage is the spirit of unity. When we learn to celebrate our unity in diversity we create an atmosphere for the glory of God to be revealed and we bring the Father joy.

Paul, speaking by the Spirit, said:

> There are different kinds of gifts, but the same Spirit. There are different kinds of service, but the same Lord. There are different kinds of working, but the same God works all of them in all men.[30]

The gifts of the Spirit are distributed among us in the body and are expressed in various ways from one person to the other. Until you come to acknowledge that it is the same Spirit, the same Lord, and the same God who is at work in others, you will not allow them to be a blessing to you and to others in the body of Christ.

Until we learn to accommodate one another, we will never be able to fully take over our world. Rather than biting and devouring one another, we should be thankful for every gift added to the body. The spirit of resentment and offense must not be allowed to reign in our hearts; we might pay dearly for it. Michal, the wife of David, in despising David as he passionately worshipped God in his dance, ended up despising God and became the only barren woman mentioned in the Bible who never had her own child (2 Samuel 6:16-23).

Simon, in looking down on the woman with the alabaster box, failed to see the depth of gratitude that overflows from a heart overwhelmed with God's mercy. Her worship was despised because Simon could only see her past, her struggles, and all she was before she met Jesus.

Judas considered it a waste because he could not see beyond the cost of the perfume of the alabaster box to the cost of her worship. He was blinded by his selfish desire. If we knew what it cost heaven and that soul to bring forth that worship, we would leave them alone. Cece Winans in her classic song "The Alabaster Box" put it this way:

Don't be angry if I wash his feet with my tears And dry them with my hair. You weren't there the night he found me You did not feel what I felt when he wrapped His loving arms around me And you don't know the cost of the oil In my Alabaster box.[31]

We can make a huge difference on the next moment of worship if only we will be willing to let the Lord have His way. Furthermore,

> Let the peace of Christ rule in your hearts, since as members of one body you were called to peace. And be thankful. Let the word of Christ dwell in you richly as you teach and admonish one another in all wisdom, and as you sing psalms, hymns, and spiritual songs with gratitude in your heart to God. Whatever you do, whether in word or deed, do it all in the name of the Lord Jesus, giving thanks to God the Father through him.[32]

Amen.

CHAPTER FOUR

MAXIMIZING OUR PRECIOUS TIME OF WORSHIP

ഇൗൕ

O ne of the greatest challenges we face is to identify just what the Father desires to accomplish in and through us during a particular worship experience and how He wants it done.

Anything less than this will cut short the measure of heaven's glory meant for that worship experience, causing dissatisfaction and sometimes frustration.

When it comes to the content of our worship, the Holy Spirit is the only one with the exclusive right to decide. He is the only bona fide Minister in Charge. Our wonderful ideas and gifts can only produce divine results when we lay them all down at the Lord's feet.

God does not respond to our worship because the performance is flawless in the rating of men, He responds to worship that is from the heart. Remember, "...man looks at the outward appearance, but the LORD looks at the heart."[1]

It is not our art that attracts the attention of heaven, it is our heart.

The entrance of a wonderfully composed musical art of mortals into the perfect worship of heaven will produce a dissonance too offensive to be tolerated before the angelic beings and the Father, but the river of worship that flows from the heart of a worshipper is enough to cause our heavenly Father to ignore the perfect praises of angels for a while. God dwells in the praises of His people (Psalm 22:3), not in our sophistication.

The first time most people heard Kathryn Kuhlman, there was nothing fantastic about her voice, but as soon as she started singing the hymn "How Great Thou Art" the whole arena became filled and charged with the presence and power of the Holy Spirit, and awesome things began to happen. Now that is worship.

What Went Wrong?

Looking at the suffocating posture of many churches today, one cannot help but wonder what went wrong. Why should people come into that which is called worship with pains, sorrows, and frustrations and then leave without encountering God?

Why should people come to church with a spiritual hunger hoping to experience a touch from God but leave disappointed?

If what we read in the Bible and have heard about the presence of God in the midst of His people is real, then what went wrong?

Why should people be made to go through this unfortunate boring experience called worship one week after another?

Something must be wrong when people have to sigh at the awareness that the next day is another time to attend worship.

Why should anyone see the worship service as a burden or a waste of time?

Why should anyone prefer to sit at home without feeling like they have missed anything when they ought to be in church?

Can you relate to these questions? What was it that happened that made you feel like the worship experience was a waste of time?

These and many other questions must be answered if the church wants to remain relevant in our ever changing and dynamic world.

The failure of the church to make the required impartation on men from one generation to another is the reason people seek for other alternatives to fill the void of their souls. Some have turned to drugs, devilish cults, and other dangerous options in an attempt to satisfy the spiritual hunger of their souls.

Receiving divine insight from the Father about every worship experience is the only way out of the woods. This may not be the popular and current desires of men, but if we will faithfully follow on, we will get unusual results.

By divine insight, we have been given the capacity to enter into the realm of the Spirit to know the things of God by the personality of the Holy Spirit, who lives in us and empowers us to provide answers to the yearnings of many hungry and thirsty souls.

Paul once wrote by divine revelation saying, "For who among men knows the thought of a man except the man's spirit within him? In the same way no one knows the thought of God except the Spirit of God. We have not received the spirit of the world but the Spirit who is from God, that we may understand what God has freely given us."[2]

It is true that we have access to understanding the things of God by our fellowship with the Holy Spirit, but except we continually surrender our will to the will of the Lord we cannot bring men to the place of worship. It is only when we are sensitive to the Spirit that we are able to deaden the distracting desires of the flesh (Romans 8:13).

Men like Paul the apostle saw how important this is, and that is why he wrote, "...I die every day...."[3] This death speaks of his willingness to yield completely to the will of the Father on a daily basis. It was another way of saying, Lord, have Your way. If we understand just what the Father requires of us, it won't take that long before the world will see His glory in us.

Kathryn Kuhlman once said, "It is not silvery vessels He is looking for; He is not looking for golden vessels. He is looking for yielding vessels."[4]

Glorious things await any soul that is passionately sold out to God.

David the psalmist once cried out to God saying,

> O God, you are my God, earnestly I seek you; my soul thirsts for you, my body longs for you, in a dry and weary land where there is no water. I have seen you in the sanctuary and beheld your glory because your love is better than life, my lips will glorify you.[5]

Seeking the Voice of Worship

Those who cannot find the presence of God in their personal time of worship will not be able to lead others to experience the presence of God in public worship. They have no business leading others in worship, but unfortunately many of them are in leadership today. For some, the passion they possess is stirred up by the drive to make more money or an opportunity to gain some fame. The worship arena is the wrong place for any man to gain prestige or make money. **If the reason you worship is wrong, your worship cannot be right.** Worship is not about you. Neither is it about your denomination or traditions. It is all about Him.

A worshipper is a worshipper any day, anytime, and anywhere, no matter the prevailing circumstances.

A few years back, in the course of going through the forty days' journey of *The Purpose Driven Life* by Rick Warren, I learnt of how the beautiful song "Heart of Worship" was written by Matt Redman. His pastor was determined to teach "his church the real meaning of worship. To show that worship is more than music, he stopped the use of all forms of music in their services for a period of time with the hope that they will learn to worship in other ways."[6] That would have spoilt the party for some, and some die-hard up-beat music lovers would have gone on vacation from this church. But for a passionate worshipper like Matt, it was an opportunity to bring to light an important awakening to the fact that worship is beyond the music—and a deeply inspired worship song was born.

Going through the text of this song, it should not take long for you to sense the call to sincere worship. There is not one time I have used this song by the prompting of the Spirit in worship that it did not stir the hearts of people to worship with a fresh passion.

This is the point we all must come to understand: worship is beyond the sound of music. It is much more than sugar-coated or flowery words. Until we are tuned to the frequency of the Spirit, it will not be possible to access the realm of worship. If we depend mainly on music or eloquence of speech to get people to worship, then we are guilty of manipulating them. We would have to go beyond emotions and reasoning to be able to stir up a true hunger to worship.

During one of the Billy Graham crusades in the UK, he was accused of manipulating the crowd to respond to the invitation to accept Jesus through the use of music like "Just as I Am." Billy Graham and his team decided to lead the crusade without singing, and amazingly the response to accept Jesus became even greater. They continued the meeting this way for some days until the people began to cry, "Give us 'Just as I Am,' for this silence is killing us."[7]

Spend quality time with the Lord and He will reveal to you the hidden mysteries and strategies to produce awesome results to His praise and glory.

Worship to some has been reduced to a well developed and strictly followed pattern. It is more about keeping up with religious activities or creeds that require men with special academic qualifications. Any worship built on human capability will soon become a burden too heavy to bear, and it will produce little or no impact on the lives of desperate worshippers. The Lord has said, "...my yoke is easy and my burden is light."[8]

Don't try to get it done by might. Just keep your mind on Him. The hymn writers advise that you:

Turn your eyes upon Jesus,
Look full in His wonderful face,
And the things of earth will grow strangely dim.
In the light of His glory and grace.[9]

Our eyes focused upon Jesus will destroy all unnecessary burdens and cause us to comprehend the ways of the Spirit, releasing in us genuine worship before God.

Giving Expression to Your Worship

During my days at seminary, I had the rare privilege to study Christian worship and other courses at the feet of Rev. Dr. Paul O. Davidson. (He was an American missionary who played a strong fatherly role in shaping my concept about life and ministry.) I learnt from him some invaluable insight about Christian worship that I believe will help us make the best of our worship moments.

Here are some insights from what he taught us. He defined corporate Christian worship as a "...**dramatic, dynamic, dialogical** encounter between the triune God of the Bible and His people in which God speaks and / or acts to reveal himself and His will and God's people respond to Him in appropriate biblical ways."[10]

This was further substantiated by the divine encounter of the prophet Isaiah as found in Isaiah 6:1-13. From the day I heard this definition, the three "Ds" caught my attention. For over twenty years now I have been involved in planning and leading worship, and I have come to see the strong relevance of the three "Ds" in worship. The worship encounter of some may not count for worship in our judgment, but sometimes an invisible and intangible impression upon a soul can lead to a beautiful expression of worship from the heart that is real and exhilarating.

Not everyone approaches worship with passion and expectancy. Some are just there to fulfill all righteousness, but if the atmosphere is right, they might turn out to be the eye of the storm.

By the use of the dramatic, dynamic, and dialogical approach in expressing the hidden passions of our heart, we are able to make others comprehend with us the divine fellowship between mortals and the Almighty, thereby making worship accessible to all.

The Dramatic Touch

From my experience of writing, acting, and directing stage drama some years back in my local church, I know how effective drama can be in conveying the gospel message. A good drama is captivating and thought-provoking. The audience is introduced to a storyline which arouses their interest, and in their curiosity to see what's next, they follow on to the end of the message.

This dramatic element was the strategy by which God arrested the attention of Moses (Exodus 3:1-6). Moses saw a bush on fire yet the bush was not consumed. So in his curiosity he said, "I must turn aside now and see this marvelous sight, why the bush is not burned up."[11] Just then the Lord called out to him from the burning bush. This was the beginning of Moses' walk with God. From this moment on he passionately served the Lord.

A worship experience with some dramatic element will help arrest the wondering minds of people and so prepare them to encounter God.

Worship leaders with a fresh passion for God are like this burning bush. They are able to make others wonder and ponder while the encounter lasts. You cannot meet them and not pay close attention. People fall asleep in church because there is nothing fascinating about the whole worship experience. A worship leader with the burning bush impact will capture the attention of the people from start to finish. Like the storyline in a good drama, the people's desire to get the whole idea will become the bait to make them carefully follow from one scene to another. They become emotionally involved with the whole experience and suddenly find themselves singing, shouting, jumping, laughing, or shedding tears. And in no time they are just where the scriptwriter wants them to be.

In our worship experiences God is the scriptwriter, the Holy Spirit is the director/producer, and the worship leaders are the star actors. The big difference is that in this production no worshipper is permitted to be a spectator. Everyone has been designed to play one active part or the other. Worship is not a spectator sport. This is why people at some point in a worship experience are prompted to dance, clap, or fall flat on the ground. When all present are part of this drama, it is not difficult for their hearts to burn with a fresh passion to worship God.

We see this dramatic element at play again in Isaiah's encounter with the Lord as found in the book of Isaiah, where it is graphically described in the following words:

> In the year that King Uzziah died, I saw the Lord seated on a throne, high and exalted, and the train of his robe filled the temple. Above him were seraphs, each with six wings: with two they covered their faces, with two they covered their feet, and with two they were flying. And they were calling to one another: "Holy, holy, holy is the LORD Almighty; the whole earth is full of his glory."[12]

> At the sound of their voices the doorposts and thresholds shook and the temple was filled with smoke. "Woe to me!" I cried. "I am ruined! For I am a man of unclean lips, and I live among a people of unclean lips, and my eyes have seen the King, the LORD Almighty."[13]

Isaiah was so overwhelmed by this encounter that he cried out without being asked, "Woe to me!"

Those who have encountered God in such dramatic magnitude are often too overwhelmed to complain or be passive. The time spent there has always been a worthwhile experience. People cannot excuse themselves from this encounter except for ulterior motives. It is just too precious to walk away from. If people can sit through a secular film for two or three hours, then it is nothing short of mediocrity that we are unable to get their attention for a two-hour worship experience. If we have to shout, threaten, or beg people to stay through a worship experience, we need to ask God for mercy.

When you lack the burning bush effect, at best people will endure your worship time. Give them a burning bush and they will turn aside to see. They will come without much trouble on your part because they don't want to be told what they have missed; they want to experience it themselves.

We can make a difference if only we are willing to allow the Lord to set us on fire. Nobody can ignore a burning bush. A man once mightily used of God in extraordinary ways by the name of John Wesley was asked how he was able to attract so many to the message of the cross, and he replied, "I set myself on fire and they come to watch me burn."[14] This is amazing.

The Dynamic Touch

In every man there is this insatiable appetite for something new, something unusual, something different from the norm. Something that adds color to life or spices up the taste and feeling we get from life. This is why people are easily drawn or attracted to the most up-to-date thing in town, even when it is so crazy and unreasonable.

Some worship experiences are just too boring or stereotyped. They lack the necessary ingredient to cause people to be totally sold out to the course. Something vital is missing. The dynamic touch is lacking. This is where I personally give kudos to Ed Young of Fellowship Church USA. He is dynamic and full of creative ideas.

Something is said to be dynamic when it is full of life, powerful, passionate, and progressive. Those involved in drama or the movie industry know too well that they cannot afford to produce anything common or boring if they want to remain relevant in the business. They are always after that which is full of life and unique. Often it is the quality of the content that makes one outfit stand out from the others. This is why they are willing to pay for quality content in the hope of having an edge over others.

If we wish to get the attention of people, then our worship experience must not be anything less. The quality of people you attract to your worship experience is determined by the quality of your impartation. The impression we give to people when they walk into our time of worship can either make them become passive or active worshippers.

Dynamic people waste no time in getting your attention. They are so captivating, so full of life, insight, and a strong drive to accomplish their dreams. They seem to have so much on the inside waiting to be expressed. Everything about them is designed to arouse your curiosity so much that you don't want to miss an episode. With them, there is never a dull moment, gloom, or indolence.

When a child of God or a church is like this, they possess the power to attract people ahead of others. When John the Baptist came preaching, he came in his own style. Here was a man terribly dressed, with an unrefined approach, but when he started preaching, people left the cities, magnificent synagogues, and the well-dressed and well-cultured leaders of the temple to hear this crazy-looking man crying in the wilderness.

It was so powerful an influence that some concluded he must be the long expected Messiah. But when he was asked, he simply said, "I am the voice of one calling in the desert.... I baptized you with water but one more powerful than I will come, the thongs of whose sandals I am not worthy to untie. He will baptize you with the Holy Spirit and with fire"[15](John 1:23, Luke 3:16 NIV).

Almost anybody can baptize you with water, but only the Lord can baptize you with the Holy Spirit and fire (the word "baptize" means to immerse in something). As we spend quality time with the Lord, we get to the place where we are immersed in Him. Please note that this baptism speaks of the Holy Spirit and then fire. Most Pentecostal preachers preach about the baptism of the Holy Spirit and then leave out the fire. It is the lack of this fire that has made many who come to worship too passive.

When the Holy Spirit overshadows us, He sets us on fire for God, and it is this overwhelming presence that makes worship dynamic. You cannot be overwhelmed by the Creator and not be creative. It is not difficult to tell if something is on fire. Whatever is on fire can be easily identified by the presence of smoke, heat, and the force or vibration it produces. So is your worship on fire?

Dynamic people have the ability to produce results where others have failed. Whenever they walk in, you immediately become full of expectation. They walk in with a glow that enlightens and liberates souls. Dead and forgotten dreams are resurrected back to life, and people are able to see a new and glorious path for their feet to fulfill destiny.

People are often amazed as they ponder the difference dynamic people have made. With the ordinary and less sophisticated, they have been able to produce a wonder in the eyes of many. The fact is that they themselves are a phenomenon too amazing to be ignored.

I once heard of a world-renowned violinist who was to perform before an audience, but somehow he could not make use of his favorite instrument. In its stead, he was given another violin that was not considered special. But by the time he was through, there was a rousing ovation. When he was asked how he was able to perform such a feat without his special instrument, he said, "The music is not from the instrument but from the soul."[16] The fire, the passion, was in his soul. It is the passion we have on the inside that determines the degree of boldness and excitement we manifest on the outside before the watching world.

If you don't have it, you can't give it. But if you work on it long enough, according to the rules in His presence, you may end up surprising yourself and others. When this happens, you will become charged up like a warhorse.

The major difference between a circus horse and a warhorse is the training they have received. The circus horse is trained to jump around to bring man pleasure, but the warhorse has been trained to charge forward in battle to bring man victory. In the book of Job, we have a very clear picture of the warhorse:

> Do you give the horse his might? Do you clothe his neck with a mane? Do you make him leap like the locust? His majestic snorting is terrible. He paws in the valley, and rejoices in his strength; he goes out to meet the weapons. He laughs at fear and is not dismayed; and he does not turn back from the sword. The quiver rattles against him, the flashing spear and javelin. With shaking and rage he races over the ground, and he does not stand still at the voice of the trumpet. As often as the trumpet sounds it says, "Aha!" And he scents the battle from afar, and the thunder of the captains and the war cry.[17]

If you put a circus horse in this position you are in trouble. The purpose of the circus horse is to amuse lives, but the purpose of the warhorse is to save lives.

When we are dynamic in our worship, we are like the warhorse charging forward and onward with a fresh passion to the rescue of the souls of men.

The circus arena creates an atmosphere for entertainment, but the worship arena creates an atmosphere for divine encounters. The goal of the circus is to bring men to a place of amusement, but the goal of worship is to bring men to a place of reverential awe. Life out there in the world is one big circus party, and this is the reason why the circus mentality is a misfit in the worship arena.

When we say worship is dynamic, it means it is full of life, powerful, and enjoys the favor of God. Make up your mind to apply your heart to your life's endeavors, and seek the Lord with all your being. Reach down for the hidden treasure buried on your inside, and one day heaven will suddenly smile on you.

Once you are able to cross from the domain of mediocrity and rest your feet on the shores of excellence, you can never be the same again. When others are struggling behind, you will be moving forward accomplishing your dreams with less stress to the amazement of many. This is when you are able to declare with the psalmist, "My tongue is like the pen of a skillful poet."[18]

This is something more than oratory and fluency. It empowers you to set the pace for others to follow. If we must take our vision to the next level, then we must be ready to go all the way because a skillful poet is the end product of both perspiration and inspiration. And don't forget: when the Holy Spirit is your senior partner, you are bound to succeed if you don't give up.

When all of these are fully employed, we begin to see mastery at work that is only common with the flow of a bestselling movie or drama. With the sensitive use of intrigues and suspense, such worship experiences are capable of holding the audience spellbound from start to finish. This is often the trademark of good scriptwriters and directors.

However, before these people are able to reach the perfect choice that will produce the desired effect, they may have gone through all kinds of frustrations and discouragements. The ordinary man will give up at this point, but those with a strong passion to succeed will keep working on it, and suddenly it will all fall into place and then the world cries out "bravo!"

When our worship is dynamic, our precious moments of worship become a priceless treasure and we want to relive the experience again and again. People will look forward to the next worship experience because they are certain something glorious awaits them. They know they have seen something beyond religion and tradition. They have encountered life and without doubt their passion has been ignited for more of God. The joy and satisfaction they get from such worship experiences cannot be compared with anything else.

The song "Breathe on Me" by Clint Brown gives us some insight into the true longing and passion of a heart taken in worship. It speaks of one not satisfied to live in yesterday's glory. We need a fresh release of the presence and power of God upon our souls to make it through every day.

God has more in store for us than we can imagine. The soul who seeks to be dynamic must make up his/her mind to be sincere and original.

Many times we copy others because of the result they have achieved, but then we fail to realize that what worked for them may turn out to be counterproductive to us. Even when some have to copy a pattern of the move of God in the life of someone else, until they find the divine touch of God they will not be able to produce the same result. What they copied is only the shadow; the real thing is the substance. Remember, "...the letter kills, but the Spirit gives life."[19]

When you carry the letter and not the Spirit, you minister death in places you should bring life and you end up wasting the precious time, resources, and strength of many lives. If you will get down on your face before God, you will find fresh inspirations that will deposit in you divine and unfailing ideas to help you succeed.

When you take somebody as your mentor, you still have to be careful not to end up as a cheap copy. There is something about you waiting to be expressed. Discover the uniqueness which the Father has given to you, and heaven will be glad to display another hidden treasure through you.

The Lord once told me, "If I have one thousand Benny Hinns, I will still be looking for more." God knows how much I love Benny Hinn, but He was trying to make me understand that the work is so enormous there is need for more hands to touch the world the way people like Benny have been doing for some time now.

We appreciate people like Benny Hinn and T.D. Jakes because each time you sit under their ministration, they make you realize it was worth it while it lasted. You too can make a difference in your generation.

Some people want to be a jack of all trades only to end up as masters of none. Should you hear them sing today, they would sound just like Donnie McClurkin and tomorrow they would become Ron Kenoly. When next you see them they have become Kirk Franklin, and at other times they have become Shirley Caesar. But the sad reality is that they have no clear identity of their own. They are at best cheap copies of the original. It is wrong to keep walking in someone else's shadow. Let God have His way and His glory will burst out of you.

Contestants in the *American Idol* or *West African Idol* TV show have their performances rated by the judges, often through the lens of the original artist whose work they have tried to reproduce. Most such artists have made their mark by being original, and others have to celebrate them. A contestant may go on to win the contest but until they are able to come out with something that is their own original work, their fame will soon fade away and they will be forgotten. It is not normal for people to look forward to meeting the shadow. You don't have to walk in any man's shadow. Be yourself and do your thing.

Don't limit God's treasure in your life. You may not be there yet but if you work on it and just keep trying you will get there.

An unfinished original is far better than a perfect copy. Should anybody find an unfinished work by Leonardo da Vinci, it would be worth a million times more than any replica of one of his finished masterpieces.

As you spend precious moments to allow God to work on you, people will begin to notice the progress you are making and with time you will be able to earn for yourself a place among the stars.

The Dialogical Touch

When we worship, we are able to do so because we have received some unusual prompting. The ability of a soul to adequately interpret this prompting will determine the degree and depth of worship experienced. The personality of the Holy Spirit happens to be the mighty influence behind this prompting which stirs in us the passion to worship.

Sometimes this prompting is communicated to us in the feeling of an unusual burden or what some may call spiritual hunger. At other times it is registered by the presence of an extraordinary peace or love. At times this may be a continual impression of a name, word, phrase, or musical tune in our minds.

Occasionally this impression will escape from our lips and so we release the first bubble of worship from the ocean floor of our souls to God.

As the frequency of these bubbles increases, in no time it will create enough ripples on the outside to make others partake of the divine dialogue as they are overwhelmed by this glorious tide. This is when the worship of one becomes the worship of all.

This divine dialogue transcends all human perception of the word "dialogue." The presence of divine dialogue is the major difference between mere religious form and true worship. This divine dialogue is the means by which our heavenly Father communicates to us His agenda for worship.

This call to worship is a continual stirring on every soul, but not everyone is able to respond appropriately to this call because the degree of our spiritual sensitivity differs from one person to another.

For some, before they are able to worship they have received billions of this type of prompting from the throne of grace, but there are a few who need only a touch and they are on their way.

All through Scripture we have noteworthy examples of various responses to this divine dialogue between God and man. Jacob was in the very presence of God and he never knew it until his eyes were opened to see a vision of angels ascending and descending on a ladder with the Lord standing above it (Genesis 28:11-12).

Jacob, together with Thomas and many others, belongs to a group that cannot worship until their eyes are opened to see (John 20:24-29). But there are those who are like the prophet Ezekiel, who though in the midst of other captives in Babylon was still able to see the heavens open, and before long he was taken in the spirit into another realm (Ezekiel 1:1-28, 3:14). While others were wailing by the rivers of Babylon, he was away in the spirit having an awesome time in God's presence.

Our response to the call to worship depends on the depth of our fellowship with God and the degree of our spiritual sensitivity.

When Moses saw the burning bush it caught his attention, and in his curiosity he turned aside to see; this was when he heard a voice calling out to him from the burning bush, "Moses! Moses!" and he answered, "Here I am."[20] In the actual sense, the divine dialogue began before there was any verbal communication.

The dictionary defines "dialogue" as "spoken or written conversation or talk." It is also seen as "a discussion between people in which opinions are exchanged."[21] When I read the above definitions, something told me there is more to it. I was more at home with the view that it is a "discussion" looking at it from the spiritual angle. I believe our encounter with the Lord is a divine discourse in which the Lord communes with us verbally or non-verbally. While contemplating this in my study, I found a piece of information which helped substantiate my understanding of the word dialogue. This is what it says: "...dialogue is from the Greek dialogos, which comes from dia-, meaning 'between,' and logos, meaning speech."[22] Therefore, there is much more happening in between our speech. It does not have to be a verbal conversation or communication for there to be dialogue.

Sometimes when the Lord initiates this dialogue, the comprehension you receive in a fraction of a minute may take over an hour to explain in spoken or written dialogue.

Let me try to shed more light on this. Some years back when I was just a religious church boy, something extraordinary happened to me which became my turning point in life. Prior to this experience I was a well-known figure in my local church. I participated seriously in the various aspects of church life. I memorized and quoted a lot of scriptures to the admiration of some, but deep down in me I knew I was empty. The best of my effort was inadequate to change my ways and life, so I finally gave up trying.

But one night as I slept I had an unusual experience that was too good to be a dream. I suddenly saw the sky open with the Lord Jesus in His glory. He wore a white robe with a red one on the sides from the shoulders. But what I will never forget is the glorious yet terrifying look of His face. In it I could see His kindness and love for me, but at the same time it was convicting me of my sins. Without saying a word in the verbal sense of communication, He had said so much to me, and without doubt I got the message. The darkness of my heart had been revealed by the light of His presence, and by the time it was all over I was so terrified I could not pray my religious prayer. By my religious knowledge I knew this to be the rapture of the saints and that I was far from being ready. I was so terrified that it was only after a while I was able to ask God for mercy.

This is the point: if you ever have an experience in which the Lord communes with you in a divine discussion that is non-verbal, without doubt you will get the message. Whenever the Lord initiates this dialogue, He intends for it to stir in us the appropriate response of worship that is in spirit and in truth.

Before there is any song raised, before there is any prayer offered, before there is any lifting of hands or bowing down in worship, before there is any message given and response to an altar call, the Lord sends this prompting to our hearts, calling us to worship. It is not by our initiative we worship, "for it is

God who works in you to will and to act according to his good purpose."[23]

A woman once caused a serious stare and some controversy when she disrupted a dinner party to pour an alabaster jar of perfume on Jesus. She went on to wet His feet with her tears, wipe them with her hair, and kiss them as she poured the perfume. Those around could not understand the divine dialogue that was taking place so they were quick to judge. Judas Iscariot could only see the waste of a very expensive perfume and the gain he would have made from it. Simon, the chief host of Jesus, became very disappointed; he could not imagine why Jesus would allow a prostitute to come this close to Him. In his heart he said, "If this man were a prophet, he would know who is touching him and what kind of woman she is – that she is a sinner."[24]

While they were busy running to conclusions, Jesus stayed with the divine dialogue that had now become an act of worship. But in all these not one verbal word was spoken.

In our worship services, before we announce "the call to worship," worship has begun in the hearts of many. A divine dialogue with the Lord precedes most of our formal worship. Due to the divine dialogue which preceded this gathering, Jesus knew that the woman was looking for this opportunity to express her heart full of gratitude to her Maker for her many sins that were forgiven. To her, the expensive perfume was the best way she could show her gratitude, and she made up her mind not to be troubled about what others would say. She was determined to pour her love on the Lord.

Many times we hinder people from truly expressing worship because we are too much in control of our worship experiences. We want everything to be just the way we want it irrespective of the divine dialogue between us and the Lord.

If we knew what it cost the Lord to bring people like this woman to the place where they are able to express their hearts in worship, we would leave them alone. Jesus had to rebuke them by saying, "Leave her alone."[25]

We must learn to mind our own business when we come to worship. Too many people are busy policing others in worship. They get so preoccupied with others that they themselves can hardly truly worship. As long as you allow yourself to be distracted by others you will cut yourself off from the divine dialogue in worship.

Until you are open and sensitive to the Holy Spirit you will not be able to recognize the prompting of the Spirit to initiate the divine dialogue that will ultimately lead you to worship.

I do not subscribe to the use of indecent and emotional outbursts, which often result in confusion and disorderliness in worship, but when you see a sincere outburst stirred up by this divine dialogue, you can't help but be moved to worship. It was the touch of the Master that stirred up this woman to worship in a profound and very intimate way.

True worship is not a monologue (a one-way speech or conversation), neither is it a soliloquy (talking to yourself verbally). In worship, the Lord gives the prompting and we are expected to respond in the appropriate way. It is a call-and-response experience.

The African and the Use of Dialogue in Worship

In the ancestral idol worship of African traditional religion of West Africa, worship has never been a monologue. There is always an active participation of the worshipper and the deity. Most of us in this region grew up to observe our fathers worship with a conscious awareness that the deity being addressed was an active and terrifying presence. When our fathers woke up in the morning, they went to a particular spot in the house to address the deity by name, often with much praise which they augmented with some sacrifice or libation.

They became very sensitive to the activities and feelings of this deity, daily watching out for signs and symbols that were often part of the non-verbal dialogue to which they must quickly respond in all seriousness. They believed nothing just happens. Others may call it superstition, but for them it may be the difference between life and death.

To those who practice ancestral idol worship, they just cannot afford to offend the gods. With them, not even the eclipse of the sun is to be taken with levity. They must consult the oracle to be sure it is not a sign that the gods are angry.

The deity is actively in charge of their lives, customs, and traditions. The presence of famine, pestilence, or other forms of hardship is often considered to be a sign that the gods have been offended.

They are always in dialogue with the gods. This is the reason why it is difficult to find a typical West African who is an atheist; a few West Africans who are atheists got it from the Western influence, and they are often considered a joke. The average West African understands the role of divine dialogue in worship. This is the reason why when they become Christians, they want to have a real and personal communion with the Lord. Their point is that if their ancestors and idols, who were considered to be of lesser powers, have been so real, then the Almighty God must be more real. That is why in the average worship centre in Africa, people are there because they want to hear what the Lord has to say. The God of the African is a talking, active, and powerful God. Anything short of this is not God, and they will not have any reason to be there.

Quiet the Flesh and Encounter Divine Dialogue

We cannot afford to be insensitive or passive to the divine dialogue initiated by the Lord to lead men to passionate worship. This dialogue often begins as a non-verbal form of communication that only becomes verbal when it has reached the climax. The prophet Isaiah was already overwhelmed by the divine dialogue before he cried out, "Woe is me! For I am undone."

Whenever a soul is taken in this dialogue, the response transcends the intellect; it comes straight from the heart. There are times when this divine dialogue is initiated by the sound of musical instruments or even silence. The sound or silence in itself may not be associated with any word, yet when sensitively applied it will play an important role in the dialogue.

This is the reason why we must be careful not to disrupt the purpose of God for a given worship experience by doing our own thing. We must not allow our flesh to become so loud that people can no longer hear the divine dialogue that is ongoing.

As we partake in corporate worship, we help to either stir or stifle the worship of those around us. This is more serious for worship leaders. When someone stands to lead the worship, the divine dialogue going on between this soul and the Lord is being played out for all to see. At such moments, the degree to which you are yielded to the Spirit will determine what will be passed on to those you are leading in worship. In other words, you can help make or mar the worship of others.

Whenever heaven entrusts us with this awesome responsibility, we must be mindful of the fact that this is God's business and we must do it His way. By the time a sensitive worship leader is through, he/she should have been able to communicate the heart of the Father to fellow worshippers.

I believe that in every worship experience the Lord intends to communicate something to His people. This is often a general message in relation to His plans for that week or season, but at other times it may be a direct word addressing the issues in somebody's life. People are forced to swallow religion and the tradition of man because those in leadership are insensitive to the divine dialogue.

Worship leaders will do well to heed this caution: "Guard your steps when you go to the house of God. Go near to listen rather than to offer the sacrifice of fools...."[26]

Be careful how you speak, act, sing, or play the music in worship; the destiny of many is in your hands. Andy Park in his book *To Know You More* says, "...a sensitive heart is so essential for each musician. If the musicians are tuned in to the dialogue between God and his church, they will sense how to accent the time through musical embellishment."[27]

We must learn to understand and follow after God's leading as we enter into the all important moment of worship. For every worship opportunity, we have so many wonderful resources in gifts and talents to choose from. It is only when we are sensitive to the Lord that we are able to make the right choice. This is why the preparation for worship begins in the place of prayer and deep communion with God. The Holy Spirit often gives us this prompting in the hope of driving us to the secret place to seek for divine guidance, but it is the degree of our sensitivity to His voice that will make the difference.

If you are busy doing several things you may not be able to get a complete revelation for that all important moment of worship, and the purpose for that meeting can be frustrated. We may have had "a nice time," but until our worship brings us to the place of deeper devotion and passionate longing for more of God, the divine dialogue is incomplete.

When a worship experience leaves us panting for more of God and causes us to lay our lives on the altar in total surrender to His will, then the dialogue for that worship is complete.

With a sensitive worshipper, the two-hour worship experience may have taken a week or more to prepare for; the worship service was only the peak of the dialogue.

When leaders are willing to pay the price, the worship will become electrifying and life-transforming.

Conclusion on the Three Ds

Isaiah was a prophet for many years before his encounter with God that we read about in Isaiah 6. But it was after this dramatic, dynamic, and dialogical experience that his life and ministry were positively transformed. My seminary lecturer and father in the ministry, Dr. Paul O. Davidson, did point out that, "The interaction between God and Isaiah can be seen to be both DIALOGICAL and DRAMATIC. But in addition, another important element, an essential aspect of the interplay, must be noted; the situation at the end of the meeting is not the same as that at the beginning. There has been a change in Isaiah's life and in the realization of God's kingdom among his people. God's sovereign power has been revealed. That same power has been revealed to transform the life of Isaiah and, potentially, to transform the life of the entire kingdom of Judah.

We can, therefore, describe this divine-human encounter as DYNAMIC."[28]

When we experience a service that is dramatic, dynamic, and dialogical, everyone from the worship leaders to all other worshippers can testify that they have encountered God.

There is no limit to what can happen in such moments. This is why the heavenly Father takes pleasure in His children and rejoices over them. The prophet Zephaniah gave us some insight into this by revelation when he said, "The LORD your God is with you, he is mighty to save. He will take great delight in you, he will quiet you with his love, he will rejoice over you with singing."[29]

The worship which the Lord rejoices over must be according to His divine purpose and plan. In such meetings, you can almost see the glow of God's glory on the faces of those present because He is in charge. When people are in this atmosphere, they are not in a hurry to leave. This was the kind of presence Doris Akers felt when she composed the hymn "Sweet, Sweet Spirit." It is said that "the inspiration for the song came during a prayer service as she and her choir felt the presence of the Holy Spirit."[30] She wrote the following words:

> There's a sweet, sweet spirit in this place,
> And I know that it's the Spirit of the Lord.
> There are sweet expressions on each face,
> And I know that it's the presence of the Lord.
> Sweet Holy Spirit, sweet heav'nly dove
> You're right here with us filling us with your love.
> And for these blessings we lift our hearts in praise,
> Without a doubt we'll know that we have been revived
> when we shall leave this place.[31]

As we walk with the Lord, may we truly experience the Lord rejoicing over us in our precious moments of worship. Amen.

CHAPTER FIVE

AN INVITATION TO THE THRONE ROOM

꧁꧂

In the year 2000, as I was approaching the end of my training for the work of the ministry at the seminary, the Lord gave me one of those unusual openings. It was so hard to believe but it was true and so real. I was in Abuja (the capital city of Nigeria) on the invitation of Mr. President (Chief Olusegun A. Obasanjo), together with other seminarians led by the head of the music department, Rev. Dr. Paul Davidson (an American missionary).

We were inside the presidential villa preparing for the dedication ceremony of the first Aso Rock Chapel. We had spent hours preparing for the ceremony that was scheduled to take place the next day. It was so serious that the rehearsal went past midnight into the early hours of the day of the dedication. We were all excited and anxious at the same time because of the enormity of the task at hand. Everything was expected to be both excellent and impactful, therefore responsibilities were assigned to those who were believed to be outstanding in their various majors.

I was amazed when James K. Ajiboye, a colleague, and I were entrusted with the privilege of leading the opening session of this service in praise and worship. The two of us had a quick preparation and it was agreed that I should take the lead. Suddenly it dawned on me that the credibility of this reputable music department of the seminary was now resting on my shoulders. I had led praise and worship at my local church and at some other gatherings for many years now, but I knew this one was somehow different.

All through that night, several things went through my mind. I considered my humble background, and it was hard to imagine that I had been chosen to play a significant role in this historic event in the life of the church and our great nation Nigeria.

Furthermore, it occurred to me that I would not just be leading the first praise and worship session in this magnificent chapel in the presidential villa, I would be leading the high and mighty of our nation in praise and worship. They included honorable members of the House of Representatives and distinguished senators, permanent secretaries, ambassadors, Mr. President, and a visiting African president. Many of these people I had only seen on television or read about from the pages of newspapers. And to think that I was about to stand before them live brought such an overwhelming feeling to me. I was not sure how they would respond to church songs. To the best of my knowledge, most dignitaries hardly respond to church choruses. In addition to all this, I realized there would be a live television coverage that would be seen all over the country and beyond. All these thoughts were making me nervous, so I decided to ask for divine assistance. I went to God in prayer expressing my concerns about leading the beginning of this very significant worship service. As I poured out my heart to the Lord, I suddenly became more conscious of His presence, and I knew I had gotten my breakthrough. I saw myself in the court of the King of glory, standing there before His throne room. All of a sudden all that filled my heart was the awesomeness of the presence of the Lord. All my anxieties and the consciousness of those important dignitaries faded away. It so overwhelmed me that by the time I stood in the chapel to lead the praise and worship, I had only one desire and passion, and that was to bring others into the presence of the Most High.

I started by saying something like, "May we all please rise in honor of the King of Kings and Lord of Lords as we praise and worship Him," and I saw everyone including Mr. President stand up to worship. By the time we were through, those I thought would feel less dignified to worship had worshipped with singing and dancing to the glory of God. But you know, you don't have to stand in the presidential villa to truly worship God with your very best. If you happen to be in an uncompleted wooden structure in a remote village with only five farmers, and you are sensitive enough to get your spirit tuned to hear the Spirit's call to worship, it won't take long before you will be ushered into the very throne room of the Father. You don't need live television coverage to experience true worship. True worship begins with our spirit open to recognize the invitation to worship by the Holy Spirit from the throne room of the King of Kings.

Once there, no other thing matters. All our focus must be on Him who sits on the throne. The moment you recognize this as an invitation for a divine encounter with the Father, it will stir in you a fresh passion to worship.

Entering the Throne Room

Here is a very good picture of an invitation to the throne room and the worship that followed:

> After this I looked, and there before me was a door standing open in heaven. And the voice I had first heard speaking to me like a trumpet said, "Come up here and I will show you what must take place after this."

> At once I was in the spirit, and there before me was a throne in heaven with someone sitting on it. And the one who sat there had the appearance of jasper and carnelian. A rainbow,

resembling an emerald, encircled the throne. Surrounding the throne were twenty-four other thrones, and seated on them where twenty-four elders. They were dressed in white and had crowns of gold on their heads. From the throne came flashes of lightning, rumblings and peals of thunder. Before the throne, seven lamps were blazing. These are the seven spirits of God. Also before the throne there was what looked like a sea of glass, clear as crystal.

In the center, around the throne, were four living creatures, and they were covered with eyes, in front and in the back. The first living creature was like a lion, the second was like an ox, the third had a face like a man, the fourth was like a flying eagle. Each of the four living creatures had six wings and was covered with eyes all around, even under his wings. Day and night they never stop saying:

"Holy, holy, holy is the Lord God Almighty, Who was, and is, and is to come."

Whenever the living creatures give glory, honor and thanks to him who sits on the throne, and who lives forever and ever, the twenty-four elders fall down before him who sits on the throne, and worship him who lives forever and ever. They lay their crowns before the throne and say:

"You are worthy, our Lord and God, to receive glory and honor and power, for you created all things, and by your will they were created and have their being."[1]

From this encounter, one can infer that spiritual vision or sensitivity plays a serious role in our ability to recognize the call to worship. Before John heard the invitation to the throne room, his eyes were opened to see in the spirit. He saw a door wide open and then he heard the call asking him to come up.

Every invitation to worship is an invitation to a higher realm, and if any man will be able to access this realm he must do so in the spirit.

Those who are able to hear this call to worship in their spirit should have no problem ascending into the throne room in the spirit. When John went, it was in the spirit, not in the flesh. Anything that is of the flesh cannot go through the door of the throne room in heaven.

Many are struggling to worship because they can't see or hear spiritually. They are trying to access the realm of worship in the flesh, and this is not possible. Until we respond to the call like John, we will never be able to enter the throne room. "...Those who worship Him must worship Him in spirit and in truth."[2] But not all have been able to gain access into this realm. This is the reason why many operate in the realm of mere religion. It does not require them to gain access into the throne room. All they need do to belong is follow some manmade rules and regulations and they are in.

Those who studied philosophy and psychology are still struggling to provide answers to the emptiness of the soul of man. The power of imagination cannot take you there; neither can religious consciousness take you there.

It is only in the spirit that we have access into the realm of worship. Worship is not a flesh thing, it is a spirit thing. When you respond with your spirit, you are positioned to encounter Him who sits on the throne.

Accessing the Realm of Consistent and Passionate Worship

John also saw twenty-four other thrones with twenty-four elders seated around the throne of God and four living creatures. But the main focus was on the one who sits on the throne. His majestic and awesome presence is all that is needed to stir up worship from the living creatures and the twenty-four elders day and night.

You cannot be in the throne room and not worship. The reason we don't always experience fresh and passionate worship is because we are not always in His presence. Our minds are full of too many concerns which distract us from being focused on Him who sits on the throne. Except we climb up and dwell in the realm of the Spirit, we will experience fluctuation in our worship. When we go from the flow of God's river into a dry riverbed in our worship experience, it is because we are walking in and out of the Spirit's realm.

If we are not connected to His presence, we cannot receive the stirring that produces fresh and passionate worship. No matter how gifted you are, something will be missing. At best you will satisfy the desires of the flesh, but those who are spiritually sensitive will know something is wrong.

In the year 1990, I started encountering God in very awesome ways that made me just want to stay in the place of private worship. During these times of worship, as soon as I said the words "I love You, Lord" I would experience a flood of His presence overwhelming me, and I would get goose bumps all over. Sometimes it would be so intimate I would feel a warm embrace, and I knew it was the Lord. It was the sweet fellowship of the Holy Spirit resting on me, and there is nothing like it. When you come to know the Lord in such intimate ways, you will not want to miss any opportunity of fellowship with Him. This is why when I began to experience some dryness and struggle as I tried to worship around the same time, I became so troubled and desperate to return to that sweet fellowship. I examined myself for sins, and there was no improvement. Then one day as I was pouring out my heart to the Lord, I felt His wonderful presence again. When my confidence returned, as I communed with the Lord, I asked Him, "Lord, why is Your presence not always on me? Why do You sometimes leave me alone?" And I will never forget what He said to me. He said, "I did not leave."

I was shocked because I wondered how I could explain the experiences I just had. I had been struggling to worship for some time now. Then He said, "You are the one who moved," and it startled me. I did not understand it. So He said this, "As long as you are in this room you feel the atmosphere of this room, but as soon as you walk out, you can no longer feel it." I got the message. The Lord did not move; I was the one walking in and out of His presence.

Worship is not by following the order of a program; it is by entering a realm.

The cares and anxieties of life, and the traditions and teachings of men will take us away from the presence of God. We must put all of these behind us and hide away in God's presence. Talk to the Lord and sing your heart to Him; He will fill your heart with life and show you the way out of the woods.

David, a man after God's own heart, once said, "You are my hiding place; you will protect me from trouble and surround me with songs of deliverance."[3] And the Lord replied to him with these words, "I will instruct you and teach you in the way you should go."[4]

What a glorious privilege.

You don't have to lose your cool. Keep your eyes on the Lord and you shall see His glory. He has promised to "...keep him in perfect peace whose mind is stayed on him."[5] Paul and Silas were seriously beaten and thrown into jail for preaching, but right inside the prison, with their feet fastened with stocks, at midnight they burst into prayers and praises to God, and the Lord sent an earthquake which shook the prison to its very foundations to set them free.

In every circumstance and situation, if you will just stay your heart in the Lord you will become sensitive enough to hear that glorious call to worship, and in the Spirit you will be ushered into the throne room of heaven where everything bows to worship Him who sits on the throne.

CHAPTER SIX

CREATING AN ATMOSPHERE FOR WORSHIP

I have come to understand that in a Christian gathering what really counts are not the names or titles we have on parade, nor the sophistication of the auditorium and equipment. An array of orators, gifted singers, and musicians and a meticulously planned agenda coordinated by an excellent protocol would be wonderful, but when all is said and done, it is the degree of transformation upon souls that counts.

There is more to worship than program schedule, methods, and doctrinal positions. Once you miss it you've missed it. If your motive is wrong your worship cannot be right.

Set Your Priority Right

In our attempt to put together something fascinating and momentous, we often neglect seeking the all important presence and leadership of the Holy Spirit. We often plan considering the things that will move men versus move the Spirit. We spend long and stressful hours having consultations with men but only a few weary moments with the Holy Spirit. We become careful not to offend men but carefree about grieving the Holy Spirit.

Our precious time, strength, and God-given resources are spent on that which will add to our reputation, name, and prestige rather than on what will further the course of God's kingdom. Instead of being moved by the urging of the Lord, we want to move the Lord to validate our agenda. Consequently, our meeting has become one big noisy party with little or nothing to show for it because we have placed the cart before the horse.

In simple English, our priority is messed up.

The Place of Surrender

If we will ever see His awesome presence and glory manifest in our meetings, then we must intentionally seek to create the right atmosphere for worship by yielding all on the altar.

Our meetings are in short supply or devoid of God's presence because we are not willing to let go of those things the Spirit of the Lord is uncomfortable with. Sin and every manifestation of the flesh will either reduce or cut off the manifestation of God's glory in our worship (Romans 3:23).

There must be a deliberate effort to live a life that is holy and acceptable to God, and when this is sincerely done from the heart, we will come to the place of surrender and His glory will be evident in our lives (Romans 12:1, John 12:24-25).

It is required that we lay down our gifts or talents before the Lord for them to be useful in His service. God cannot be glorified by that which we refuse to lay down before Him.

Is there something you have not surrendered to God? This may be the very thing preventing you from entering into your glory and destiny. The earlier you lay it down the better for you because in life every second counts. Abandon your life, your cares, and your gifts to Him and you will be amazed at what He will do with you. He is able to cause you to bud and blossom in the most unusual ways like Aaron's rod (Numbers 17:7-8).

As we willingly decrease for Him to increase, surrender from the heart to the Lord becomes a reality and we simply want to live for His glory. This is not religious fanaticism, neither is it salvation by our works; it is living a life full of God's grace and peace.

The writer of the hymn "Take My Life and Let It Be Consecrated" gives us an idea of a heart sold out to God in the following words:

Take my life and let it be
Consecrated, Lord to Thee;
Take my hands and let them move
At the impulse of Thy love,
At the impulse of Thy love.[1]

Hearts like this are often a great asset in worship, and whenever they are present it is not difficult to experience true worship.

The Lord desires to manifest His presence in all our meetings, but the degree of this manifestation is connected to the degree of our hunger and surrender. This is where those who have yielded themselves to the Master are invaluable in the manifestation of heaven's glory. When we learn to yield all to the Lord we will see His glory like never before.

The Culture of the Kingdom

To be able to touch lives beyond the intellect is not in our human abilities. Our skill with languages, theology, psychology, and theories is not sufficient to bring down the glory. This is exclusively the work of the Holy Spirit.

Our culture, temperament, dispositions, traditions, and ideas of man should not define for us the acceptable ways to express Christian worship. We have a more excellent way in the leading of the Holy Spirit, who is always in conformity with the Word of God as revealed in the Bible.

By following the leading of the Holy Spirit, we are able to introduce men and women to the culture of the kingdom of God, and His glory is revealed for all to see.

Worship is not enshrined in the religion and traditions of men. The religion and traditions of men are unreliable because they are susceptible to the influence of human philosophies and culture, which are unstable and fallible, but the Word of the Lord endures from one generation to another.

When we go after God with enough hunger and passion, He will overwhelm us with His presence and bring us to the place where we are able to catch glimpses of the glory of the kingdom. Once there, we are able to comprehend the life and the culture of the kingdom. This is where the content, form, and expression of our worship are truly defined. We are then able to manifest on earth that which is in heaven and so invade earth with heavenly realities to the glory of God.

When we step out, it should be to accomplish the will of the Lord and not our own ambitions. When the Lord taught His disciples to pray "Your will be done on earth as it is in heaven"[2] He revealed to us the true passion of His heart. He wanted them to see they could manifest heaven on earth, but that it had to be a genuine passion from that heart to God.

Whenever we choose to step out with a "wonderful idea" that is not initiated by the Lord, we will not see His glory. Our wisdom, skills, experiences, and theological understanding are just too inadequate to reveal His glory. The more we try to show what we are made of, the further we are from the manifest glory of the Lord. "By strength shall no man prevail."[3]

We must passionately seek Him and so make the world see His glory. To seek the Lord is to seek the glory. Until you know the Lord you cannot know His glory. It is the lifestyle of the kingdom to walk in His glory; to live otherwise simply confirms that you are none of His.

His Presence Is Everything

In a live praise and worship recording of the album *We Speak to Nations* by Hosanna! Music at Lakewood Church, the Lakewood choir did a beautiful rendition of the song "Everything" by Israel Houghton. The music is beautifully arranged, but it is the message of the text that captured my heart. I like the emphasis on the fact that God is everything. It expresses the true passion of a worshipper. Those who consider the Lord as their treasure and priority have this hunger for more of God. You may touch any other thing in their life, but don't make the mistake to mess with the presence of the Lord because they will fight you with all they have got.

King David once cried out, "My soul followeth hard after thee...."[4] The prophet Habakkuk in his resolve said, "I will stand upon my watch and station myself on the ramparts; I will look to see what he will say to me, and what answer I am to give to this complaint."[5] And Moses in a passionate plea to God cried out, "If your presence does not go with us, do not send us up from here."[6]

If some of us had heard the Lord saying, "I will send an angel before you and drive out the Canaanites, Amorites, Hittites, Perizzites, Hivites, and Jebusites"[7] we would have been so excited and thrilled that an angel was going with us to deal with our enemies and give us the blessing we have been praying for all these years, but not Moses. For those to whom worship is a shopping mall (just a place to get more blessings from God) this would have been alright. They will in fact celebrate this as a wonderful breakthrough. In churches where the major emphasis is on getting the blessing rather than knowing the giver of the blessing, this declaration would have been received with a thunderous "Hallelujah!"

A blessing without the presence of God is a curse. Check out Lot, the nephew of Abraham who thought he was very smart when he chose the well-watered valley of Sodom and Gomorrah over the divine covering he had abiding with Abraham and you will see better (Genesis 13:8-11).

Lot thought he got a blessing when he settled for Sodom and Gomorrah, but it was a curse. He later had to run out of Sodom for his dear life, but by this time his wife had become a pillar of salt and his daughters later committed incest with him (Genesis 19:15-38). Why would they do such a thing? They learnt it from the wayward lifestyle and culture of Sodom and Gomorrah. Many have been reduced to a crumb of bread because they left the presence of God.

Those who are after the blessing and not the presence of God would have been satisfied with God's promise to the Israelites that He would send an angel to take them to the Promised Land, but not worshippers like Moses.

Moses was sensitive enough to observe that the Lord had said at the end of this promise, "But I will not go with you..."[8] and immediately he knew something was wrong.

When you have an intimate relationship with somebody, you are able to see beyond their words to feel the content of their heart. You are able to perceive when they are just tolerating you, and if this relationship means anything to you, you will abandon every other thing to settle the issue.

Moses could not imagine life without the presence of God, and that's why he persisted with the Lord. I wish we all could be patient and sensitive enough to be sure of God's presence before we jump at some flowery opportunity. Actually, the root of our problem is far down in our hearts, for "...where your treasure is, there your heart will be also."[9]

Our heart's desire is the guide of our steps and the passion behind the achievements of our soul. Many have traded the presence of God for fame and fortune only to end up miserable. If you are travelling down this miserable lane, you can stop right now and cry out to God and He will bring you out.

Moses remembered that it was the presence of God that made the difference in Egypt, their deliverance from the hand of Pharaoh, the opening of the Red Sea, and the victory all through their journey. These were only possible because this awesome presence was with them, and now it would be foolish to try to make the rest of the journey without this presence. This presence was the true identity of Israel and without it there would be no Israel.

I know of places where the people started with a strong hunger and total dependence on the Lord, but after a few successes they became too confident and began to trust in their wisdom, methods, gifts, and skills. They suddenly felt they knew what to do, when to do it, and how to do it. As long as they were still getting results here and there, they failed to see the need to passionately seek God. That which began with the fire and glory of God was gradually reduced to mere religion and tradition, "...having a form of godliness but denying its power."[10] They lost their true relevance.

Like Moses, once you have tasted the intimate and awesome presence of the Lord, it is foolish to settle for anything less.

Passionate worshippers like Don Moen understand the importance of this presence. Through his song "May Your Presence Go with Us," a fresh passion for God's presence is being rekindled in the hearts of many like never before. There is no substitute for the presence of the Lord. Without Him you are nothing.

Those who celebrate the gift of God over the presence of God are more concerned about the praise of man than the favor of the Lord. Their value is in the applause of man rather than the approval of God. Worshippers like Moses would rather cry out, "...if you are pleased with me, teach me your ways so I may know you and continue to find favor with you...."[11]

When we cry out to God like Moses did, we will be positioned to receive the greatest assurance: "My presence will go with you and I will give you rest."[12]

Without the presence of the Lord our worship experience will become lifeless, empty, and full of struggles, and we will not be able to make any tangible impact. Only the presence of the Lord will reveal the glory.

Having a Foretaste of Glory

More often than not, those who enjoy the manifest presence of the Lord in their public meetings had a foretaste of what is to come during their private time of fellowship with the Lord before they stepped out.

After such experience, they are able to stand before others with boldness and confidence knowing that it was a concluded issue. They have had a glimpse into the glory that is to come, and they know for sure it will happen.

Oral Roberts in the days of his healing campaigns would often wait to feel the presence of the Lord before he stepped out to preach with great passion for the healing of many. His ministry was one filled with a lot of amazing results because he had a foretaste of what was to come. I have heard him testify that as he expectantly waited on the Lord, an unusual presence would come upon his right hand and by this his faith would be stirred up to see the sick healed.

No worship experience should be approached with levity. We must seek the all important presence of the Lord to go before us and with us. When the Spirit takes over our souls, everything He envisions us with will become possible.

We know from Exodus 33 that Moses went on to not only get the assurance of God's presence, he also had the rare privilege of seeing the Lord pass by him as the Almighty revealed His back form. This was the closest anybody could get to the glory in the Old Testament after the fall of Adam.

This awesome presence in the camp of the Israelites caused their enemies to become too frightened to stand against them. When we tarry long enough in God's presence, the world will see His glory in us and testify that God is with us.

Empowering the Spirit Man

We are all created with a free will but only the will that is continually yielded to God experiences true liberty and glory.

Adam was the crown of God's creation, but he lost the full weight of the glory intended for him by disobedience. When Adam was created, God made him a living soul (Genesis 2:7). His intellect, will, and emotions were perfect, but as for his spirit there was still much to receive in the place of fellowship with God. As his spirit man became empowered in the presence of the Father, he became more spiritually sensitive and less sensual. If this had continued long enough, his spirit man would have assumed the dominant role of leading the body and soul in the issues of life and the worship of God.

Through the spirit he would have been able to willfully yield his entire being in worship to God the Father. Then Adam would have come to the place where he was totally engulfed in a greater glory to the admiration of the angelic beings. This spirit-dominated life would have made the difference in his first spiritual battle in Eden, which his intellect and emotions could not withstand. The intellect is disgracefully erratic when it comes to spiritual issues, and only a fool would depend on it in the battles of life.

When we fail to spend quality time with the Father, we become susceptible to the tricks of the enemy. Unfortunately, this is when we often think we know what we are doing so we suffer a shameful defeat.

Falling Under the Power

Our times of worship are actually times of spiritual renewal. They are opportunities for us to be transformed as we encounter the awesome glory of God, but not many get it. Each fellowship with the Father at the cool of the day was designed to usher Adam into a greater glory, but it only lasted for a while.

The manifest glory of man was meant to be greater than that of the angels, but after the fall mortal man could not stand the presence of angels. There are scriptural accounts and other documented evidence to back this up. When these angels showed up, men like Ezekiel, Daniel, and John had to be given supernatural strength to stand on their feet.

This is simply because whenever angels appear, they come wrapped in the awesome glory and power they were decorated with as they tarried in God's presence. This is also one of the reasons people fall under the anointing during worship experience. Our frail being suddenly encounters the supernatural presence of God, and as our system is overwhelmed we buckle and fall. Any man who has spent quality time soaking in the anointing of God's presence will also have men and evil spirits overpowered under their ministrations.

The more we dwell in the presence of the Father, the more we become like Him.

Your Generation Is Waiting for You

Every one of us has been carefully thought of before we were assembled together and delivered to our generation. God our Creator took time to put in place the things we need to succeed in carrying out our divine assignments (2 Peter 1:2-3).

Those who spend quality time with the Father are often visited by a divine wave of glory that helps to lift them into a realm and consciousness of life in the Spirit ahead of others. This is where they are able to access divine mysteries. When this is obvious in the life of someone, we say he or she is anointed.

This is how a man like John was able to write the book of Revelation. It all became possible because John entered into another realm. He said, "I was in the Spirit...."[13]

Before men like Ezekiel and Daniel were able to share the deep things of the Spirit, they were bombarded with overwhelming visitations and encounters that took them to the realm where they could handle such things.

When a man is able to enter into this realm, he becomes the envy of his generation. He leaves such lasting impressions in the hearts of men that it makes them crave for more of God. Such persons are not after a form, they are hungry for an encounter with God. When we are able to walk with God in such a way that fascinates others, it will become much easier to draw men to love and worship God.

The world is able to ignore so many religious houses because there is nothing extraordinary going on there. They are just like secular organizations, clubs, societies, and the like.

I tell you the truth, if any man is able to walk into the other realm where life in the Spirit is made manifest, he will find out that the hearts of many are not as hardened as we assume.

Years back when I was just a religious Baptist boy, I was very active in my church programs and in the various organizations where we thought a lot about our denominational heritage and Bible stories. We were required to memorize and quote some scriptures to be able to move to the next stage of our religious journey. By reason of this I became very religious and was able to recite a number of scriptures from memory.

But then, back at school, I came in contact with a Christian (though only from a distance) and something happened to me. There was this unusual glow I noticed on him that made me very uncomfortable with my religious life. He did not say a word to me, yet I got convicted of my sins and suddenly realized there was more to Christianity than what I had. It stirred in me a craving to know God more. I became spiritually hungry to have what was on him, and when I got it I knew it and this brother became my friend.

Beloved, your generation is waiting for you. There is more about you waiting to be made manifest to your generation.

When we truly worship Him in spirit and in truth, before long those who come in contact with us will begin to desire the God in us. By simply appropriating the awesome grace of God for our lives we can enter into this place of glory. It is available to all—the choice is yours.

It is true that by the fall of Adam we inherited a fallen nature, but by the redemption of Christ Jesus we can now have divine access to the throne of grace and become partakers of His divine nature and power (2 Peter 1:3 and Hebrews 4:14-16).

It is possible that men around us have their hearts hardened to God because we have not been able to make them encounter the glory of God through our lives. If they can see and admire it, they will desire it. Your generation is waiting for you.

CHAPTER SEVEN

PREPARE AN ATMOSPHERE SATURATED WITH LOVE

❧❧❧

I am yet to find a place where people freely worship God in spirit and in truth that is not saturated with love. Love is one of the most important factors in creating an atmosphere for worship.

Wherever the people deliberately work to saturate the atmosphere with the love of God, it is easier to worship there. In places like this, people feel secure to express themselves in worship. There is no sense of apprehension or compulsion in the atmosphere. It is a free flow of the sincere passions of the heart, making it easy for one to respond in love and heartfelt devotion to God. Most of what we call worship today lacks this all important ingredient of love.

In an atmosphere saturated with love you are not motivated by religious sentiments but by intimacy with God. In an atmosphere of intimacy people reach out to God (in a vertical flow) and to man (in a horizontal flow) as they worship joyfully and willingly.

In this place, observers can tell this is not just some form or tradition. In this atmosphere, the Almighty God who some consider unapproachable can now be seen as a loving Father reaching out to us for a loving embrace.

As in the parable of the prodigal son, our heavenly Father wants us (worship leaders) to prepare a feast for those coming back home. He wants us to clothe them with His finest robe (righteousness), put a ring on their hand (spiritual identity and authority), and shoes on their feet (equipping and empowering them to transform their world wherever they go).

The Father also wants us to celebrate their homecoming with the killing of the fattened calf. What could be this fattened calf? This can be anything set aside for special use or special people (Luke 15:11-24). This means we don't have to make them go through unnecessary stress just to gain the approval of man when they have been accepted by the Father. Subjecting people to certain requirements and the judgment of man or an organization has often left many feeling ostracized rather than welcomed.

Our legalistic approach to worship is one reason why some people see God as a stern, unapproachable, and unappeasable being. The Father's arms have been stretched wide open all the while to welcome them into the family, but they could not see it because some sanctimonious folks got in the way.

In an atmosphere saturated with love, those who come in feeling unworthy and condemned are shocked to discover the depth of the Father's love for them. This is when the God they once dreaded and would rather view from afar suddenly becomes the love of their life.

Most people often wonder about what God thinks and feels about them, but the truth is that most of the time the only answer or clue they will ever have to this question is in the kind of reception we give to them.

A warm reception from other worshippers has always been a great impetus to assist many to let loose their first expression of true worship. The reason why some people are only at home in certain places and with certain persons is the kind of reception they get.

Most of us who have tasted rejection and condemnation can testify that it dealt a terrible blow to our self-esteem or personality, and once we are out of such an atmosphere we don't want to go back there. Once we are able to find a place saturated with intimacy and acceptance, we will find it difficult to be at home somewhere else.

Many pastors and church leaders trouble themselves to track down their members because they have not been able to create an irresistible atmosphere of worship. Some of these leaders are unable to create this atmosphere because their major emphasis is on vainglory, selfish pursuit, and denominational and traditional views.

The BSF Worship Experience

In the early '90s, I was part of one of the most outstanding examples of a fellowship saturated with the love of God. Amazingly, it was all happening in a Baptist church. This was not a result of the traditions or teachings of the Baptist denomination; it was the response of God to the hunger and sincere passions of some young desperate souls.

Prior to this experience, there were many occasions I left this church's worship service unsatisfied. It was too focused on intellectualism, which was not satisfying my spiritual hunger. My heart was yearning for a sweet fellowship saturated with the life of the Spirit, but this seemed continually elusive and my patience was running out.

When some of my Pentecostal friends got to know where I worshipped, they advised me to find another church where the Holy Spirit was freely moving. As I poured out my frustration to the Lord in prayer, He told me, "You don't have to leave." He went on to show me in a vivid vision of the night that a revival was coming to this particular church, and about a year later it began. God visited this church in various amazing ways, and all the religious hindrance began to fall apart. During this period the door was opened to a group called the Baptist Student Fellowship (BSF). With the assistance of some Spirit-filled university students the foundation was laid.

Much of the emphasis was on the watchword of the BSF, taken from John 13:35, which says, "By this shall all men know that you are my disciples if you love one another."[1]

This BSF fellowship became saturated with love, and within a few weeks the membership grew from less than fifteen people to an average of fifty to sixty people in weekly attendance. Within three years of its existence this gathering of young people fellowshipping for just ninety minutes had over a hundred hungry souls in its weekly attendance. They came from Anglican, Apostolic, Roman Catholic, and Pentecostal churches to experience God in a Baptist church.

The news soon spread like a wildfire all over the city and beyond, and when some doubted they were simply told "Come and see"[2] just like Philip said to Nathanael when he doubted the possibility of the Messiah coming from Nazareth. Amazingly, some who came to see found it difficult to return to the religion and lifeless worship they left behind.

People began to develop an intimate relationship with God and a pure love and appreciation for one another. The personality of the Holy Spirit became a strong reality, and many got saved, healed, and delivered from demonic afflictions.

During our worship time, the presence of the Lord became so real you could feel it in the atmosphere and see it in the sweet expressions on the faces of those present. There were times it became so overwhelming that some could not help but scream, and this got some of the traditional guys fuming, but it was hard to contain this ecstasy. On several occasions some church leaders came to the venue of this fellowship threatening to put an end to it, but the Lord made it impossible for them to do so.

The leaders of the BSF were summoned to answer questions and threatened again and again, but it was not strong enough to intimidate them because they were ready to serve God at any cost. The passion to worship had been kindled in our souls and all the cold water of hell could not quench it.

So great was the move of God that some parents asked the BSF leaders to reach out to their teenager, and there were amazing results as many lives were transformed. Yet other parents were skeptical.

In this awesome move of God we saw young people who used to avoid church become so hungry for God they were often at the place of fellowship at 3 or 4 p.m. waiting for a 5 p.m. fellowship.

It is not true that young people don't like church; the truth is that they cannot stand lifeless religious forms.

During the years of this BSF fellowship, I saw that at the close of each worship experience it was difficult for many of these young folks to leave. Compelled by a genuine love, some would stay behind to check on others with various problems ranging from academic to social and spiritual issues. At other times it was simply because we were rejoicing over the testimony of somebody as the joy of the Lord flooded our hearts.

On some occasions it took the anger of certain church leaders to disperse the people in their various clusters, only for them to regroup in some other ways. The love that held this BSF together was so amazing because most of the people could not wait till the next Friday for the fellowship. They had become hungry and passionate for more of God.

There were many occasions when, without a scheduled meeting, one after the other, some fellowship members came visiting till we had eight or ten people in my home. We often spent the time studying the Scriptures, and it was with great delight. When someone got a new insight to a scripture, he or she would say, "God gave me this rev" (meaning a new revelation), and we would rejoice in the sharing of this new revelation. At other times we would watch a video message of leading preachers like Benny Hinn and others.

As we fellowshipped together, you could tell how desperate we were. With rapt attention we participated as though the worship service was a live experience. As we watched this recorded worship, the presence and power of the Lord showed up in my home and glorious things began to happen.

These were glorious days that resulted from an atmosphere saturated with love. It was not the place or the denomination involved that made this huge difference. It was the hunger of souls desperate for more of God, and it created an atmosphere the Lord was pleased to identify with. It was an atmosphere saturated with love.

In 2007 I went to minister at the church of a close friend and brother, and after the service he said to me, "I am yet to experience the kind of fellowship we had in our BSF days." But you know, deep inside of us we began to sense that God was about to do it again and this move would be more glorious than the former. Hallelujah!

People are becoming more dissatisfied with what is happening in many religious gatherings in the name of worship. The hunger for more of God and true worship in spirit and in truth is stirring up so many, and they are seeking for a place to encounter God. As soon as they find one they will settle down to worship.

The Lord Himself is at work. He is leading souls to the places where they will encounter His awesome presence and glory. It is happening even now; don't be left out.

Keep Your Eyes on Jesus

You cannot help but worship if you keep your eyes on Jesus. I am yet to meet a soul who truly encountered the presence of the Lord with an open heart that did not become a worshipper.

In the presence of the Lord, the covering cast upon the hearts of men will melt away like wax before the fire. The love of God is like the fire that both refines and transforms.

When people come to an intimate knowledge of the Lord, worship becomes an avenue to express the true affections of their heart. Just listening to the songs of worship by some persons will reveal to you how much they love and cherish the Lord.

Songs like "There Is None Like You," "Jesus, Lover of My Soul," "Amazing Love," "Lord, You Are More Precious than Silver," "I Love You Lord," "As the Deer Pants for the Water" and many others were not written to win any award. They are the true expression of the love relationship between a worshipper and the heavenly Father.

It is easier to make men see the glory and beauty of the Lord as we freely express our heart of love to the Master through song than through any other means.

If we will lead people to focus on Jesus, in no time they will be transformed in the light of His glory to become intimate and passionate worshippers.

Too often we try to teach men to worship by focusing on sectional doctrines, traditions, methods, programs, and religious rites. We then wonder why we get little or discouraging results. The truth is that until they are able to see how much the Lord loves and cherishes them, they will not be sure of committing their hearts to the whole thing.

Often when people walk into a place of worship, they come in with a lot of apprehension. They will only let down their defense as they are overwhelmed by this irresistible love. Until they encounter the love of Jesus, they cannot enter into the realm of worship. Worship is a spiritual business which requires a spiritual response from the heart.

When the prophet Isaiah encountered the Lord, he saw Him high and lifted up in His glory, and Isaiah felt so unworthy to stand in His presence, but after he received the cleansing by the coal from the altar of God, he was able to enter into this realm of worship and deep communion with God (Isaiah 6).

Our number of years in the ministry has nothing to do with the realm of worship we occupy. The degree of our hunger, vision, and intimacy with the Lord will determine how far we can go with God in each encounter.

The more you know Him, the more the fascination and admiration you receive to worship. Whatever happens to your vision will determine the passion you express in worship.

Worship leaders often help to create the only vision some people will ever see of the Lord in worship. Whatever we say or sing about often influences their understanding and response in worship. This is why great care and sensitivity to the person and leading of the Holy Spirit is so important.

Certain songs help to saturate the atmosphere and minds of people with the presence of Jesus in worship, and we need to pay attention to them. Keith Green's song "O Lord, You're Beautiful" is one song that so easily moves me to respond in intimate worship. The lyrics say it all:

> O Lord, You're beautiful,
> Your face is all I seek;
> For when Your eyes are on this child,
> Your grace abounds to me.[3]

The response of a particular group of people to worship is strongly influenced by the teaching they have received consciously or unconsciously. The Word of the Lord says,

> Let the word of Christ dwell in you richly as you teach and admonish one another in all wisdom, and as you sing psalms, hymns and spiritual songs with gratitude in your hearts to God.[4]

Some years back I accepted the invitation to minister at a particular church, and I went there with a lot of expectation hoping to have a wonderful time, but I was shocked by the response of the people to worship. There was this dryness in the atmosphere.

As I led them in prayerful singing, I soon noticed that nothing had changed, so I opened my eyes and was amazed to see eyes staring back at me. Some looked angry, as if God had offended them; others were indifferent. No hand was lifted in worship, and some stood with arms akimbo or crossed, just waiting for me to be through. I immediately knew there was no way one could effectively minister in such an atmosphere.

As I poured out my heart to the Lord, He made me see that they could not express their hearts in worship because their hearts were held captive by religious form, tradition, and other concerns. They needed an intimate encounter with the Lord, and somebody had to help take them there.

When people have mere religious and traditional knowl-edge, worship is approached from the viewpoint of what their group, denomination, or tradition says. Anything outside this is often resisted.

I came to understand what I was dealing with, so I started sharing more about Jesus and His wonderful love for us. As soon as they got the message the atmosphere was gradually transformed until it got saturated with the love of Jesus, and the people began to express their hearts freely in worship. The difference was like that of night and day. Life came into the place and people began to worship with enthusiasm. Some were moved to the point of tears, and others could not help but lie down in total surrender to God.

When you see a group of people express themselves in worship, you can have an insight to what they know, believe, and adore. The Lord Jesus said in Matthew 6:22 that "the lamp [light] of the body is the eye..."[5] and if our eyes are focused on Jesus, who is the light of the world, we can never dwell in dark-ness. The more we focus on the Lord, the more we become like Him. We are then able to see the depth of His love for us, as demonstrated through His death on the cross to bring us eternal life. We are able to see the immeasurable grace and glory He gave to us by making us children of God's kingdom with great privileges.

To any soul that has come to know this, just the mention of the name "Jesus" is enough to stir up a strong passion to worship. Jesus is the sweetest name to this soul. Just the very thought of Him is life and peace.

To this soul worship is like a flowing stream. This worship is beyond the use of flowery words that are crafted to appeal to the intellect. It is the cry of a soul that is awestruck, and sometimes such worship can only be expressed with unintel-ligible exclamations.

Here is a soul mesmerized and consumed by the glory of God struggling to translate this ecstasy to comprehensible words. Whenever hearts that truly love the Lord open up their mouths in worship, the atmosphere is different. Others present can tell this is God because they feel the surge of the glory imparting their souls.

People come to church hoping to encounter God during our worship, but it is unfortunate that many pastors and worship leaders stand in the way. I don't think if they are in search of a good performance they will even think of our church. They came to church to see Jesus and that's it. Please let's give them Jesus in our songs, in our prayers, and in our sermons, and they will be fine.

John the Baptist had an outstanding reputation with the people. Some saw him as a prophet of God, and others even thought he was the promised Messiah. He had the opportunity to make himself popular but he chose to point the people to Jesus instead (John 1:19-31).

Like John, when people are drawn to our success, we must be careful to point them to Jesus, and if we do He will glorify His name and the worship will be fresh and passionate.

When the atmosphere is charged with the presence of the Lord, the worship leader will not have to struggle to minister and it will become so easy to get people to respond to God. This is the reason why the Lord must be the focus of our worship services from start to finish.

If we talk too much about ourselves, our organization, or our denomination, they will begin to see more of us and our imperfections and we will cut them off from the move of God. Then we will struggle to worship.

Not everything is needful in a worship experience. Some things can be ignored or attended to at other times or in other ways. All our energy must be focused on making Jesus the center of attention. Then it won't be so hard to create an atmosphere saturated with love, and people will develop a natural affinity to worship with fresh passion.

CHAPTER EIGHT

THE FRAGRANCE
OF INTIMACY

Pretense is a mockery of the originality and true beauty enshrined in any soul. To uncover pretense in worship is to discover a stench too offensive to be tolerated before the Father of spirits.

The true beauty of any soul is revealed when that soul is lost in sincere and deep intimacy with Jesus. Most people are head over heels about falling in love, but there is nothing compared to falling in love with Jesus. When a soul is lost in communion with Jesus, this intimacy will produce a sweet fragrance with such pleasantness and eternal impact that cannot be ignored. As this soul burns in passionate worship, an aura of honesty and transparency becomes visible.

The soul that is truly conscious of the awesome presence of the Most High has no need to pretend. When surrounded by His glory, our hearts overflow with sincere gratitude and expressions of love too wonderful for words. It is in this place the Father reaches down with love so amazing, and the soul is transformed and lifted to a higher dimension of life.

It is in this place the power of the flesh and the dominion of sin are crippled. Burdens are lifted and darkness becomes light. There comes an illumination too great for ignorance to remain, and the soul is liberated as our spirit soars on the wings of the Spirit.

It is here the confused and frustrated find perfect peace and the lost and lowly find a place at His banqueting table, where His banner over them is love. It is in this place of intimacy that many find the grace to distinguish themselves in their generation. Once this grace is released on them, they are able to send the fragrance of this intimacy even to generations unborn.

By this fragrance, Noah was able to attract the favor of God upon his life, his family, and the rest of the human race. God smelt the aroma of the sacrifice Noah offered in worship and was moved to terminate the curse over the ground and establish a covenant with him and every living creature. It was by this covenant we have the promise that water shall never again destroy the whole earth, and the rainbow became the token by which God reminded Himself of this covenant (Genesis 8:20-22, 9:1-17).

By this fragrance, Abraham distinguished himself as a friend of God and became the father of many nations (2 Chronicles 20:7, Romans 4:17-18). It was this intimacy that made it difficult for God to keep His top-secret mission about the destruction of Sodom and Gomorrah from Abraham (Genesis 18:17-18).

By this fragrance, David captured the heart of God and became known as **a man after God's own heart.** So much was the depth of this intimacy that when God needed someone to lead His people He said, "I have found David my servant...."[1] Israel needed a king but God found a worshipper in the bush, and the fragrance of this intimacy was strong enough to enthrone his descendants as kings forever. So great was the honor that even Jesus the Messiah is identified as the son of David.

By this fragrance, Daniel got extraordinary results in prayer to the amazement of all; this was in the place where astrologers, magicians, and all the wise men of Babylon toiled without success (Daniel 1:19-20, 2:27-28). The fragrance of this intimacy caused him to remain relevant through the reign of four kings: Nebuchadnezzar, Belshazzar, Darius, and Cyrus (Daniel 1:21).

By this fragrance, John the beloved disciple was able to survive the wicked reign of the Roman emperor, and while in exile on the Island of Patmos he became the vessel by which the awesome book of Revelation was written (John 1:1-3,9).

The fragrance of his intimacy with the Lord positioned him to receive this deep and timeless mystery from the Lord. There cannot be a better ear open to hear and a better heart open to receive the secret of the Lord than that of the man whose head in intimacy found a resting place on the bosom of the Lord, near to the heart of the Master (John 13:23).

Nothing else can reveal the true beauty of a soul as when that soul is truly intimate with God. For it is only when we continually see in our mind's eye the beauty and glory of our God that we are transformed to manifest His image and likeness as a sweet fragrance to the watching world.

Making a Difference between the Living and the Dead

In the Old Testament, one of the strongest symbols of worship is the altar of incense located just before the veil that leads to the ark of God. The high priest did not enter into the most holy place without the incense. If he did, he would be as good as dead. Before going beyond the veil, he took with him a censer full of burning coals which created a cloud of smoke with a sweet-smelling fragrance that went before him to settle over the mercy seat. As the Lord smelt this fragrance the priest was able to obtain favor from God. Until this was done, it was impossible for him to make atonement by the blood on behalf of the people.

The various rituals that took place just before the offering of the incense would not have been adequate to take the priest beyond the veil. The sweet smell from the incense made a huge difference between life and death.

In a similar way, our worship expressed through songs of intimacy from sanctified hearts to the Lord may well be the sweet smell of the incense we need to obtain favor in the presence of God. It is the most effective means of obtaining divine favor.

In Numbers 16, the Lord got fed up with the rebellious attitude of the Israelites and became so angry that as He spoke with Moses, a plague broke out in the camp. As the plague moved from one tent to the other the people dropped dead. It happened so fast it left them with no time to go through the normal process of entreating God for mercy. Something had to be done and it must be done swiftly and effectively. This was when it occurred to Moses that the best antidote would be the sweet-smelling fragrance from the incense. He immediately told Aaron the high priest to take the burning incense and run into the camp to make atonement for the people.

As Aaron ran toward the camp, he could see people dropping down as they died of this plague, but immediately he got in the way of the plague with the incense. The plague stopped and so "he stood between the living and the dead...."[2]

I believe the fragrance from the burning incense taken from outside the veil that leads to the mercy seat was useful in reminding the Lord of His merciful kindness, and the angel of destruction had to sheathe his sword.

So many people may be dying around us today because the church is failing in her responsibility to produce the much needed sweet fragrance that should shield her parishioners in a cloud of mercy. Some worship leaders are just too insensitive during corporate worship. It is wrong to announce, "Let us rise up and take a few songs while we wait for our guest speaker." The danger here is that these songs of worship are only being used to while away the time, and once the people get used to singing just to fill a vacuum they will gradually become passive and insensitive to the divine dialogue between them and the Father as they worship with songs.

Even worse, some pastors will go on to say as they introduce the speaker, "Now the moment we've been waiting for has finally come." May God have mercy on us and help us to see that not one part of our worship experience is insignificant. When there is effective planning by the worship leaders and a humble disposition toward engagements by guest ministers, there will be no need for such blunder. Also, serious and careful consideration must be given to the choice of words we employ in transitory statements, prayers, and singing during worship, else our altar of incense will become cold. A cold altar of incense will not be able to produce the much needed fragrance of mercy to shield the people from deadly plagues. This is why many are dying of sickness and diseases spiritually and physically. If the plague must be stopped, then we must stop playing church and become sensitive enough to give priority attention to quality and intimate worship.

It's an Everlasting Love

When you are in love with someone, you go all out to win their heart. After this is done you are able to spend quality time with your love. In our walk with God, the key word is intimacy. Anything short of intimacy is a mere religious form.

In the place of intimacy, we are able to give back to God that by which He drew us to Himself. We are able to come to the place where we begin to comprehend the essence of it all. By virtue of this intimacy our soul is integrated into the nature and purpose of the one who made us in His image and likeness.

From the onset, our walk with God was intended to be a love relationship that ushers us into greater realms of glory, and this is why the evil one tried to truncate it at its infancy, but his wicked scheme was not good enough to change the nature, plan, and purpose of the Father. God revealed the depth of His love for us when He said, "I have loved you with an everlasting love; I have drawn you with my loving-kindness."[3]

When He said "I have loved you," He wanted us to see that He made up His mind to remain committed to the love relationship no matter what happens. It is an everlasting love. We are able to walk in love not because we decide to, but because He draws us with His loving-kindness. In spite of the unfaithfulness of man, the Father remains faithful in reaching out to man for a love relationship. And somewhere, somehow, this mortal man is able to enter into an intimate relationship with the Father. "We love him because he first loved us."[4]

Those who boast of their self-righteousness are only ignorant of the Father's initiative in bringing us into a divine fellowship, and so they deprive themselves of the grace of God. We are only able to yearn for Him with a burning passion because He is at work in us.

When the Father said "I have loved you," He actually chose to be patient with the inadequacies of mortal man. He wants us to know that our failure and insolence are not strong enough to deter Him from coming after us with His love. It is an everlasting love.

You Can Tell It Is Worship

Worship is the expression of intimacy between the Father and the man He created in His image and likeness to fulfill His purpose.

It is the fragrance of this intimacy that stirs in our heart a longing to be with the Father. We should want to be with Him because we love Him, not because we have to pray or carry out any other religious obligation. Prayer is not meant to be a well-rehearsed recitation; it is meant to be the true expression of our souls in worship as we commune with the Lord.

If prayer is a well-rehearsed speech then oratory will translate into fervency and efficacy in getting answers from God. That means the unlearned and the slow of speech will have a hard time getting answers from God, but because God's throne is a throne of grace, any hungry and passionate heart can come and encounter Him.

Our preaching, praying, giving, and other expressions of our hearts must be seen as part of the content of our worship. This is the reason why it is wrong for the song leader to say after singing a few fast songs, "Let us now go into worship." It makes me wonder, what have we been doing all this while?

All we do must be seen as a vital part of the divine dialogue in worship. We all have a serious responsibility to see to it that when we come before the Father, every second counts as we try to encounter true worship.

Until you experience a personal, intimate communion with the Lord from your heart, you have not worshipped. You may have been at the worship service and really did not worship. I don't care about the name written across the entrance of the place of meeting, you still have to encounter God yourself.

That you are a Pentecostal, evangelical, or whatever is not a guarantee that what you just went through was worship. The form without the heart is not different from a social function of the Lions Club.

Church worship is more than a lineup of activities. A well-planned liturgy is not a guarantee that worship will take place. When we are more particular about the liturgical appropriateness of our worship with respect to our denominational doctrine than the will of the Father, our experience will be far from worship.

So many have come out of what was called worship wondering if it was worth it. They went in desperate, hoping to experience the reality of God, only to leave discouraged and frustrated. Something vital was missing and they knew it.

To a soul with a genuine hunger for the reality of God, your fight over liturgical appropriateness is useless. Just let them see the reality of Jesus and that will be enough.

Just before the beginning of Jesus' earthly ministry, all the religious activities of the temple, the traditions of the Jews, and the theological arguments of the Pharisees and Sadducees were the admiration of many, but after they encountered Jesus everything changed. The fame and impact of Jesus' ministry soon attracted men from far and wide because He was ministering to their soul's desire. There was something unusual in the way He taught the Scripture and touched lives. It was the first time many heard of a God who can be so intimate and personal.

The Greeks were known to intellectualize everything before it could be accepted, but a few days before the popular

Jewish feast of Passover, some Greeks came to Philip and said, "Sir, we would like to see Jesus."[5]

Whenever people encounter the glorious personality of the Lord, they will abandon all other lifeless religious gatherings and reasoning just to be in God's presence.

The fragrance of our intimacy with the Lord is all we need to attract men to worship. So many souls have been crying "we would see Jesus," but they have been disappointed with what we call "worship" because they only heard about Him but never encountered Him in our worship.

When a soul meets with the Lord, you don't need to do much theological explanation to make them worship passionately; they will know Him far beyond the doctrine of man.

When a man encounters the Lord, the veil over his heart is removed by the fire of love that now burns in his soul. Suddenly darkness is turned into day and the man who could not understand the Scripture before this experience is now filled with much zeal to study and live it. This is because he has not only met the Author, but he is continually being enthralled by a love relationship with the Author, who now lives in him.

For him, reading the Scripture is like reading a love letter from the lover of his soul, and praying is a sweet opportunity to commune with the one who loves him so dearly. To this man, worship is not just another religious activity, it is a great delight. All who come in contact with him can tell that this man has more than religion.

In the days of Kathryn Kuhlman's meetings, so many went to the meetings with skepticism and bias, but when it was all said and done they left with much life and glow. The presence of the Lord on Miss Kuhlman was just too awesome for them to ignore. Those who were apprehensive about what members of their denomination would say about attending her meetings soon forgot about their concerns. They were saturated with love and overwhelmed by the glorious power of God. They knew without doubt they had been walking under open heavens, and worship became the only natural response from these souls touched from above. In Miss Kuhlman's meetings, strange and awesome manifestations were very common, but the most amazing of them all was the transformation that took place in the souls of many.

When we are in this place of intimacy with the Lord, the sweet fragrance of our intimacy with God becomes the worship the world sees ascending to heaven like a cloud of incense. People are attracted to a relationship not a religious form.

And the Big Boys Came to Church

Oftentimes our various dispositions in church are the result of our preconceived ideas about worship. There are certain religious gatherings where it seems as if there is an embargo on the expression of joy. The faces of the worshippers are often stern and their mood too organized.

The spirits of those in this worship service are only permitted to respond in unison with other worshippers in a particular manner, and doing something different from the tradition could be considered a sacrilege.

In the 1980s, a brother in Christ was so moved by the Spirit in the middle of a very traditional church worship that he knelt down to express his heart to God. But by the time he was through, he found himself outside by the road. Some traditional enthusiasts bundled him out of the church, far enough not to constitute a nuisance to their tradition.

Many Christians today have problems with the expression of intimacy in worship. People like this have consciously or unconsciously chosen to imprison themselves in worship. They are too much in control of themselves in worship. Such persons are often so conscious of their denominational traditions and doctrine. Some others are too conscious of their class, title, office, fame, intellectual positions, and what others will think about them and their actions in worship.

During worship, if we fail to forget our ego we will become insensitive to the precious invitation from the Father to come as children to an intimate time of fellowship. Many of us have lost the element of that first love, which was full of intimacy and passion for the Lord. Over time we have become the "Big Boys" among other worshippers.

Before we got that title or position, we were sincere worshippers. But not long after we were blessed with this lifting we assumed the Big Boys status. This is what somebody called "the deacon posture." Have you observed that most deacons and church elders assume a particular posture in church that seems to confine them to a very formal role in worship? This is also applicable to many pastors.

When we become too conscious of our standing with men, we lose touch with our standing with God. Our heads get subtly swollen with pride and we unconsciously begin to struggle to worship God because we desire recognition among men. We become too dignified to bow and worship.

Oblivious to the danger of our posture, we create an obnoxious atmosphere that stifles the worship of others around us. Instead of saturating the worship atmosphere with the precious, sweet fragrance of worship, we pollute the worship with the stench of our flesh.

We must learn to humble ourselves under the mighty hand of God when we come to worship. We must not allow the little blessings of life to prevent us from worshipping God in spirit and in truth. If you are truly blessed you acknowledge that God is your source and passionately honor Him with your life.

A songwriter once wrote, "Lord, I give You my life, I give You my soul, I live for You alone...."[6]

Without the Lord we are nothing, no matter the prestige we have with men. The best recognition ever is for God to call a mortal man "son." Whoever stands before God conscious of any other status than the father-son relationship is in wrong standing.

When Jesus was baptized, the Father thought of no better way to introduce Him to the world than to call Him "...My beloved son...."[7]

Again, at the Mount of Transfiguration, He affirmed it by saying, "...My beloved son."[8]

What a privilege and honor for the Father to call you "son." Son here does not speak of gender as in male and female but of our privileges and standing with God in the Spirit. Any worshipper who understands this will gladly approach the Father mindful of the father-son relationship. He is not ashamed to cry out "Abba Father."[9]

To some this is childishness, but this is where they got it wrong and the "Big Boys" mentality crept in. There is a huge difference between being childish and being childlike. Jesus once said, "I tell you the truth, except you change and become like little children, you will never enter the kingdom of heaven. Therefore, whoever humbles himself like this child is the greatest in the kingdom of heaven."[10]

Some people who are afraid of losing their dignity are quick to label intimate worship "childish." But on the contrary, Jesus said the one who humbles himself like a child is the greatest in the kingdom of heaven.

It is the Spirit of Christ in us that stirs us up to cry "Abba Father" (Romans 8:15). This is also an indication that we have a true closeness to the Lord. The soul that cries out "Abba Father" does so in recognition of the fact that God is the source of his/her life. The word "Abba" means source, and this soul is actually crying out because it is overwhelmed with the consciousness that the Almighty is his/her source.

The apostle Paul said, "Because you are sons, God sent the Spirit of his Son into our hearts, the Spirit who calls out, 'Abba Father.'"[11]

When John the beloved wrote the book of 1 John, he began with an invitation to come experience the reality of the intimate fellowship that is available to all who are in Christ Jesus (1 John 1:1-4).

As he pondered the overwhelming revelation of our divine adoption into the family of God, he was moved to exclaim, "Behold, what manner of love the Father hath bestowed upon us, that we should be called the sons of God...."[12]

What an honor and privilege for us mortals on this side of eternity to be called the sons of God! This is the highest title anyone can have. The best the prophets of old could get was "servant of God" or "friend of God." No angel was ever called son. The book of Hebrews says that Jesus "...by inheritance obtained a more excellent name than they..."[13] [the angels]. It goes on to question, "For unto which of the angels said he at any time Thou art my son...?"[14]

What an honor for a mortal man to share in that which angels from glory cannot obtain. To every soul who truly acknowledges and enjoys this great privilege, worship has become a natural response of intimacy with the Lord. Such souls have seen that the love of the Father knows no bounds, and the cry "Abba Father" truly reveals the overwhelming gratitude of their heart.

A true worshipper often feels so indebted to the Lord; therefore anything or any means can never be too much to express this gratitude to God.

As Kathryn Kuhlman put it, "we have nothing to give Him but our love."[15] Our Lord Jesus said the greatest commandment is to "...love the Lord your God with all your heart and with all your soul and with all your mind."[16]

When we gather as His children, it is an opportunity to show how much we love Him, and we ought not to be ashamed to do so with passion.

I will forever be grateful to God for intimate worshippers like Benny Hinn. Most of Benny's meetings are saturated with worship songs that convey the sincere gratitude of our heart to God. They include worship songs like "Father, I Adore You," "Glorify Thy Name," and "Alleluia." But I want you to see the text of one of the songs he loves that means so much to me. It is titled "Holy, Holy" by Jimmy Owens.

Holy, Holy (3x)
Lord God Almighty
As we lift our hands before You
As a token of our love,
Holy, Holy (2x)[17]

We can never love or thank God enough for the love He bestows, the peace He gives, and the grace and mercy He lavishes upon us. If we by our effort truly deserve any of these, then we can boast in our strength. But we know too well that we are who we are by the grace of God (1 Corinthians 15:10). A grace so amazing that we cannot help but worship the Father in great delight.

The rest of our lives unto eternity will never be enough to show Him how much we love Him. So don't let one more hour go by without expressing your love to Him. Let your worship rise to Him as a sweet fragrance of love, for He is worthy of our worship.

CHAPTER NINE

PRECIOUS TEARS OF HALLOWED MOMENTS

We humans are deep and complex creatures with so many mysteries that are only unveiled occasionally by our words or actions. The shedding of tears is one of the most profound ways by which the deep emotional feelings of the human soul are expressed. Tears convey to the outside the deep feelings of the spirit of a man, giving a clue about the state of that heart. The degree to which a man or woman is moved to tears sometimes reveals to others the degree of compassion he or she has toward a person or thing. Prior to the resurrection of Lazarus from the dead, the deep emotional feelings of loved ones expressed in tears played a very significant role. Those present saw the tears of Jesus and immediately realized the love He had for Lazarus (John 11:33-35).

Through the shedding of tears, deep-seated feelings of frustration, bitterness, gratitude, exhilaration, and other emotions of the soul are revealed. If the shedding of tears does truly convey the deep-seated feelings of our heart, then there will be times when the expression of our tears should count as worship. More often than not, tears are indicative of an emotional relationship between one person and another.

Therefore if we truly have an intimate relationship with God there will be moments of tears.

When God created us in His image and likeness, He left something in our nature that pulls us to Him and Him to us. This is why it is possible for somebody to sit in an atmosphere of worship without saying a word, yet the teardrops from his eyes will reveal the worship going on in his spirit.

Right there, so much transformation has taken place beyond the imagination of many. When God in human form (in the person of Jesus) shed tears by the tomb of Lazarus, it was an opportunity for man to see the depth of the Father's love for mankind (John 13:35).

In an atmosphere of worship, tears are often a tangible hint of the visitation of heaven upon a soul. The story of many has assumed a dramatic twist after such an encounter. In worship, more often than not the shedding of tears is an expression of love or gratitude. Those who truly worship are not so far from tears.

It's an Expression of Intimacy

In our relationships with close friends and family members, some of the deepest affections of our souls are expressed with tears. When a child loves and cherishes somebody as they do their mother or father, nothing in the world can take the place of the one they love.

If by some circumstance they become separated physically, their souls will continually go out to one another. And when they reunite, their deep love for one another is often expressed with tears of love. This was exactly what happed when Joseph revealed his identity to his brothers after many years of painful separation triggered by horrible feelings of hatred and jealousy. He tried to conceal his affections from his brothers for a while, but after much intrigue and pretense, the day came when the floodgate of his love and compassion for them overran his game plan and he let out a cry so loud that all in Pharaoh's palace heard him. This was not the "big boys" kind of thing. It was the soul-rending and heartfelt kind of cry.

And it led him to embrace his brothers in love and joy. Kissing each one of them, he wept the more (Genesis 45:1-15).

Such hallowed moments usually produce a sense of liberty and peace. As we can see in verse 15, at the end of it all they were able to talk freely with Joseph.

Once again, when Jacob and his son Joseph were reunited after many years of painful separation, we see how precious such moments can be. They hugged and kissed each other as the tears flowed. Joseph, who was then the prime minister of Egypt, lost consciousness of his position, title, and influence and wept like a baby (Genesis 46:29).

For every heart that is passionate for God, the release of tears in worship is a sweet expression of intimacy. It is like saying, "You mean so much to me, I miss You so much." If you are truly in fellowship with the Lord nothing and no one can touch your heart like He does.

It's an Expression of Gratitude for Unmerited Favor

Sometimes the busyness of life and the craving of the flesh can draw us away from our precious moments of fellowship with the Father, till we are carried far away from His loving embrace and protection. This is when we begin to lose our peace, and soon we are left feeling empty. Right here, the soul who truly loves God begins to feel some desperation and longing to go back to the peace and contentment they once enjoyed.

This is only possible because God in His mercy lavishes much love and grace upon us over and over again. He just will not let us go. Just to know the Lord is doing this in spite of our shortcomings is enough to stir up deep emotions of gratitude within us for His unfailing love.

The precious, comforting, and loving embrace of the Lord has a way of making the heart become tender and sensitive. It enables us to anticipate and yearn for the constant abiding presence of the Lord. In this place, we do not struggle to pour out our heart to the Father in worship. It is a joyful expression of gratitude from a soul deeply indebted to a merciful and loving God.

It's in Our Makeup

There is nothing too important to lay down when you really love the Lord. This is where women are far better than men because they are more open and so much more emotionally sensitive. It is easy for women to express their love with deep emotions, and they don't mind letting go the floodgate of tears. Women relate more with their heart (emotional), while men relate more with their head (analytical).

A woman wants you to know how she feels, and she wants to know how others feel, but a man wants you to see the logic in the whole thing. Maybe this can be attributed to the fact that when God created man, the man's major assignment was administrative (Genesis 2:15), but when He formed the woman her major assignment was to meet the emotional needs of man. Her mission is to eliminate loneliness from the world, so she was made a help meet, a suitable helper. She became man's companion, and there cannot be true companionship without compassion (Genesis 2:18-23).

This may be the reason why when a new spiritual concept or move comes to town, the women are the first to lend their support to it. While the men are taking time out to investigate and analyze it, the women would have long settled down to business. You may say this is the reason why women are so gullible, but it is also the reason why so many men lag behind and sometimes arrive too late.

It's the Touch of the Almighty

I have observed that in a corporate worship experience, before most men will have their hands raised, the women are already on the ground with their faces covered with tears before God.

Whenever you find a man shedding tears in worship it is because something extraordinary has happened to him. God must have touched him somewhere to cause a serious dislocation from his natural tendency to always be in charge. When he felt the power behind the touch of his Lord and Master, he became obedient as a dog to its master. Men only submit to a greater and higher power.

This reminds us of the man Jacob (Genesis 32:1-26). Just before he had an unusual touch from the Lord, he was trying to outsmart everyone (Laban, Esau, and others), and he even wrestled with God. So when the Lord touched him and the hollow of his thigh fell out of joint, he cried out, "I will not let you go unless you bless me."[1]

Like the man Jacob, most men who are free to express themselves in worship must have been touched by God in a very powerful and sensitive way. And such men are often dependable worshippers for the rest of their lives because each limping step they take (as a result of the dislocation they have suffered) serves as a constant reminder of the futility of trying to wrestle with God.

If you are the one in this position you must have come to know that it is wiser for you to cooperate than to struggle with God.

When God calls us to a place of worship, He really intends to bless us, but like Jacob we want to prove we are men. Our wrestling with His purpose often causes us unnecessary delays and painful experience that could have been averted. If we open our hearts to Him we will enjoy the favors from His presence.

It's an Expression of Total Surrender

Too many pastors struggle to encounter true worship because they are always conscious of being in charge during the worship time. They are busy giving commands and keeping watch to see that every one of their commands is followed to the letter.

Some are too conscious of their position as the spiritual father of those they lead in worship, thereby failing to acknowledge the one and only Father in worship.

When it comes to worship, it is required of all (including leaders) to approach the Father humbly as His children. When we come willing and broken, it is no longer a struggle to worship. We have ourselves come, expecting to experience the move and glorious presence of God like every other worshipper, and so we are positioned to encounter true worship.

When the pastor of a church is a passionate worshipper, the glory and power of God will not be scarce in this worship experience. It is in awesome moments like this that words become inadequate to express the feelings of love that overwhelm us, and we break down in tears. Every believer should at least once in a while come to this point where words are inadequate to express the glory you feel inside.

Pastors who love to be in charge only succeed to cut short or hinder the manifestation of the glory of God for that worship experience.

It's an Expensive Token from the Heart

Those who cannot understand the place of tears in worship may become offended in an atmosphere saturated with deep intimacy. Like Simon, they are quick to rubbish the worship of the woman who came with the alabaster box. They are disappointed that their leader did not take charge over the situation by restraining those they consider to be too emotional.

This woman's worship was too precious for the Lord to ignore. It was a precious and hallowed moment of worship.

Her heart of gratitude was expressed with tears that were enough to wash the feet of the Lord, and she went on to dry them with her hair. As if this were not enough, she kissed His feet while adding perfume. This is true worship. In the Scriptures, one of the original translations of the word "worship" is to kiss the feet. Others could not see her worship, but the Lord did.

When she was through, the Lord made those present to see that what she did was her way of showing gratitude for her many sins that were forgiven (Luke 7:40-46). He said, "I tell you, her sins—and they are many—have been forgiven, so she has shown me much love. But a person who is forgiven little shows only little love."[2]

If you cannot see what it cost the Lord to make a soul break down in worship, you will not understand why they worship the way they do.

The degree to which we express our gratitude in worship is proportionate to the degree of our love and admiration for Him. So when next you see a soul break down in worship, don't be quick to rubbish their worship. You don't know what it cost the Lord to bring them this far. There is more to worship than your concept and comfort. Let God be in charge.

You Can Have More Than an Affair

There is more to worship than our desires and feelings. Matt Redman in his song "Heart of Worship" drew our attention to the fact that worship is all about Jesus, not us.

Some people who claim to have fallen in love will turn around and say it was all a mistake and that it never should have happened. The truth is that it was only an affair, an infatuation, not a true love relationship.

An affair is often by the spur of the moment and very sensual, lacking integrity and the total devotion of the heart and soul. It seeks to gratify the immediate untamed and malicious passions of the flesh, which soon disappear like a mirage. The more you try to get a grip of it, the further it slips away. It is so elusive and very unreliable. The more you try to make it work, the more you invest into it—and vague is the promise it holds for you. Before your very eyes the whole thing fades away, and sometimes it ends in shame or some unrecoverable loss.

He who lives in an affair will have to maintain some distance to keep his false hope alive. Deluded by this infatuation, many never get to experience true love and joy.

But he who has more than an affair has his whole body, soul, and spirit ravished and consumed with an eternal devotion and satisfaction. He/she is committed to the relationship through the stormy and fair weather. It is an unconditional fidelity that can be very transparent to all, and every attempt to grasp the substance of it will be rewarded by a rich and deep affection.

In the worship of God, we must go beyond an affair to a love relationship that is genuine and intimate. The devotion of our God to the relationship is with much sacrifice and love that cost Him His one and only Son. That is why it will be unfair for us to respond to it with little or no commitment.

In our worship, it must be all of us or none of us. And when it is all of us, you will discover that moments of precious tears are not scarce. This is because each time you come with such devotion you find that there is more mercy, more grace, more love, and more care than you ever imagined released from the Father upon your soul.

Some still struggle to accept God's loving embrace, and so they never get to know the peace and freedom of the soul lost in worship.

It's a Cry to the Love of Our Heart

When we lift up our hands in worship, we demonstrate total surrender to the Lord and Savior of our souls. It is an expression and token of our love. We are acknowledging the presence of the Father, and like little children we are reaching out for His loving embrace.

As a father, I can relate well to this. When my kids were much younger, there were times when they came to me with arms open wide and lifted up. At such times all that child wanted from me was a loving embrace. Even when that child said nothing, I got the message.

Sometimes this may be due to the fact that they were feeling tired or sleepy, but most of the time it was just a way of saying "I love you" or "I miss you," and this was often with a tender hug embellished with a big smile. At this point I became moved to say something lovely to that child, and, I tell you the truth, right there that child found favor with me. This was when my wife would often give the child a big peck. Whenever they came like this, they were just too adorable to be turned away. You just can't ignore or resist them.

If we who are mortals cannot ignore such gestures of love, then our heavenly Father will do far more with His children who lovingly come to Him.

It is the desire of our heavenly Father that we come before Him with much love and total surrender. He wants us to love Him with all our heart, with all our soul, and with all our mind (Matthew 22:37).

Most of the time it is the Father who beckons us with arms open wide, calling us into His loving embrace. But when we decide to come, it is unfortunate that we choose to come like the "big boys." Instead of extending our hands to the love of our life, we casually stroll in and say, "Hi, Dad!"

We have become too big for that babyish thing because we fail to see that with God you don't ever become too big to respond to His outstretched hands.

Jesus gave an illustration to help us understand the heart of the Father during His lamentation about the lukewarm attitude of Jerusalem to God when He said, "...how often I have longed to gather your children together as a hen gathers her chicks under her wings, but you were not willing!"[3]

To understand the message, you have to understand why the hen gathers her chicks under her wings.

When the hen stretches out her wings, she often will do so making a specific sound. By this she expects her chicks to come running to her for protection or just to give them some food, warmth, and a resting place under the covering of her wings. More often than not, you will see them running to the mother hen. This depicts a beautiful and healthy relationship between the hen and her chicks. But it is sad that those who claim to be the children of God have become too big to dwell under the shadow of the Almighty (Psalm 91). In Africa, it is said that "the chicken which refuses to heed to the call of the mother hen will soon become lunch for the hawk."

The Father wants us to come into His loving embrace and feel the warmth of His love for us, but we often want to go the opposite way.

If we will listen carefully, we will hear His voice calling us to come under the shadow of His wings as we spend quality time with Him. We need to feel His presence, listen for His voice, and just love Him. If we will continually come before the Lord like this, not even the strongest storms of life will be able to steal our peace (Isaiah 26:3).

We fret and become anxious because we have wandered far away from under the covering of His wings as we play the "big boys." It is time to come back home.

When Our Maturity Becomes a Bane

There are those who believe that worship should always be very formal and mature. For them, worship is a well-organized liturgy with predictable and fixed procedures. To speak of somebody weeping is something they consider too emotional and indecent. They boast of being able to control their emotions as a thing of pride, and this is what they call maturity, but this is an error.

Such persons give their children and others the impression that being emotional is a sign of weakness and immaturity. The truth is that they are only being proud of their insensitivity to the Holy Spirit, and they have become oblivious to their negative influence on others in making them become insensitive to the presence of the Lord.

There are some to whom worship is a thing of convenience. It is an opportunity to identify with certain classes of people to help improve their social status. In such places, intellectualism and wealth are highly esteemed and dead religious rites are celebrated above spiritual hunger and intimate relationship with the Father. It is only an affair that seeks to satisfy their fleshy desires, and it is both shallow and self-centered.

If you find them passionate, it must be about those religious activities that support their traditions, doctrines, dogmas, and denominational beliefs. When they are in such atmosphere, they put on a form of godliness and are very eloquent in the use of religious language, but outside this arena they are an apology to the body of Christ. This is deception and fallacy of the highest order. This is not worship. If our Lord and Master could weep in public (John 11:35) then it must be an error for us to think otherwise.

Worship Is an Issue of the Heart

There is more to worship than our doctrines, traditions, and concepts. There is no way our finite mind and limited reasoning can adequately and accurately contemplate the subject of worship. It is only by the Spirit that we are able to catch glimpses of the truth about worship as we yield our spirit to God.

Remember, worship is in spirit and in truth. Worship is an issue of the heart that can only be accessed in the realm of the spirit.

This was the major difference between David and Saul. David was always conscious of the divine presence of God, but Saul was more of a sensual man and at best a religious person.

When the prophet Samuel confronted King Saul for disobeying God in failing to destroy the Amalekites, Saul was armed with a wonderful excuse. On the other hand, when the prophet Nathan confronted King David for his adulterous affair with Bathsheba and the murder of her husband Uriah, he did not play the "big boy," he cried out in repentance, "I have sinned against the Lord."[4]

Saul the "big boy" ended up in frustration and woe (1 Samuel 16:14, 31:1-6). But David ended up with the mercy of God upon his life and an unusual promise to have his descendants on the throne over God's people.

When you take a look at the life of Saul, you will discover that times of personal passionate acts of worship with hands lifted or prostrating before God were scarce; he did only the religious thing. He never wrote a song to celebrate God's goodness. But as for David, there are enough records to show his love for God. He worshipped before God with all kinds of postures and expressions. Most of the awesome chapters of the book of Psalms attest to the fact that he was a worshipper.

He worshipped God with dancing till he became naked. It was so passionate that his wife had to rebuke him. She could not imagine her husband, the king, behaving in an undignified manner. Well, her reaction was no surprise; she was the daughter of King Saul, the "big boy."

Saul was a religious man, but mere religious worship does not get our spirit soaked with the presence and power of God. Without the Spirit he was unable to overcome the rebellious nature of the flesh, and it became easy for a tormenting spirit to take over his mind. But David continually sought after God and could not stand not having the Holy Spirit in his life, not even when he sinned against God (Psalm 51:11-12).

People can afford to get offended when a soul passionately worships God in spirit and in truth, but I tell you the truth, the very first time they stumble into an atmosphere saturated with God, and the glory of God is able to gain entrance into their heart, they will become so awestruck they will begin to weep.

Most people cannot worship because their hearts have not been taken. Once a heart is taken, it is easy for worship to flow out of that soul. Worship is an issue of the heart.

The songwriter summarized it this way, "Lord, I give You my heart, I give You my soul, I live for You alone...."[5] And when our hearts have tasted true worship, we will cry the words of Israel Houghton, "To worship You I live, I live to worship You."[6]

To those who are open to God from the heart, worship is a precious hallowed moment, and nothing is too great to offer to God in worship.

CHAPTER TEN

PARCHED LANDS AND THIRSTY SOULS

꘎

There is nothing like water to a dry and thirsty land. If you have ever seen a land so affected by drought the ground begins to crack, then you can truly appreciate the blessing of water.

In the remote parts of sub-Sahara Africa and the Middle East, the availability of water is a huge issue due to prolonged dry seasons. As such adverse weather conditions persist, both humans and animals are forced to move out in search of greener pastures.

The drying up of rivers, streams, lakes, and wells, coupled up with the absence of rain or the morning dew, often makes it impossible for any land to sustain the life of plants and animals. Eventually the plants will begin to wither, and after a while the land will become desolate.

Most animals are wise enough to understand the shift in the atmosphere and quick to migrate to other places with favorable weather conditions before it becomes life-threatening. If they ever have to return to their former abode, it is only when they are certain the weather condition has become favorable.

These animals can sense the danger that waits those who fail to move at the right time; therefore, as soon as they sense the shift of the season in the air they are on the move.

Even little creatures like the butterfly develop a very sensitive instinct to sense the shift in the atmosphere to know when to move, but with us humans, only a few can perceive the shift of the season and the coming of a spiritual drought.

Sometimes when these animals and insects travel, they need to cover long distances across the boundaries of nations and even continents. This journey is often through very dangerous routes where they might fall prey to both man and other creatures that lie in wait to take advantage of their migratory habit. This notwithstanding, their passion to survive has become a driving force strong enough to propel them to take the risk of their lives.

Acknowledging the Needs of Our Land

Any land blessed with adequate water supply should be blessed with adequate food production. And wherever there is adequate supply of water and food you are sure to find life and growth. This is often the destination of migratory creatures. In this place they are able to settle down and produce their young because right here the survival of the next generation is guaranteed.

Many houses of worship have become desolate because they lack the spiritual water and food to nourish the souls of man. Those who used to worship decided to move in search of greener pastures to escape death by starvation. But if the leaders will acknowledge their need and humbly cry to God the story will be different. The most effective remedy for parched lands is the opening of the heavens for the release of rain, and only the Almighty can do that. As the rain returns, the seeds and roots of plants that were buried in the earth during the drought will begin to sprout again for growth and multiplication to follow.

God can open the floodgates of heaven over an individual or a particular church after a sincere and passionate cry from the heart (2 Chronicles 7:13-14). He is gracious to pour water on thirsty souls, and desolate places of worship can flourish unto overflow. This is the promise of the Lord:

> For I will pour water on the thirsty ground, and streams on the dry ground; I will pour out my Spirit on your offspring, and my blessing on your descendants. They will spring up like grasses in a meadow, like poplar trees by flowing streams.[1]

What a blessed hope and promise! All that is required of us is a sincere cry from our heart to God. Our worship is dry and desolate because we have not been able to get the attention of our Father in heaven. There is enough rain for every thirsty ground. All we have to do is ask. When we become desperate enough for the visitation of God, something extraordinary will happen. He will bless us unto overflowing and we will see the next generation spring up like grasses in the field. We will see vibrant life, growth, and steady multiplication.

When Spiritual Drought Persists

When we choose to live in continuous disobedience to the Word of God, we move God to close the heavens above us till it becomes as hard as brass (Leviticus 26:18-19, Deuteronomy 28:23), and when the heavens are shut over any land the rain or dew is withdrawn from it and a devastating drought follows.

When Ahab the king of Israel led Israel to rebel against God by raising up an altar to Baal, God was moved to shut the heavens over his domain and there was no dew or rain in Israel for three years (1 Kings 16:31-33 and 17:1). The spiritual drought finally led to a drought in the natural realm. The rain and dew ceased, and after a while the rivers, streams, and brooks were all dried up and the drought became severe (1 Kings 17:7).

Though it took the prophet Elijah only a simple pronouncement to move God to withdraw the dew and rain, when it was time to turn it around it wasn't that easy. He had to engage this drought in a spiritual battle. Two steps were taken to cause this turnaround. First of all, he had to bring the people of God to a place of repentance. This was only possible after the contest with the prophets of Baal on Mount Carmel where it became obvious that the God of Elijah was supreme. They all fell down and worshipped, confessing that Jehovah is God (1 Kings 18:1-18).

Secondly, he went up the mountain and bowed down to the ground to labor in prayer. This he did seven times before he finally got the breakthrough. A cloud appeared in the sky as small as a man's hand, but it later grew into dark clouds accompanied by wind which caused a mighty rain to be released over the land (1 Kings 18:19-40, 41-45).

If we will truly repent from sin, our God is able to terminate every spiritual drought over our lives as the heavens open up to release rain over our land.

Restoring the Dew of Eden

When the Almighty made man, He never intended for him to experience any kind of hardship. He placed him in a garden watered by a river, and He also sent enough dew to water the ground (Genesis 2:6-10).

But when mankind fell, the human race lost the favorable condition of the Garden of Eden and was released into a dry and harsh spiritual climate saturated with sin and the forces of darkness. From that point on, mankind began to live in a state of apprehension and a mood of despondency.

The eviction from the garden was a separation from an intimate fellowship with God. From that point on mankind became estranged from God, and for the first time he experienced struggle as he tried to commune with the Father.

He who once had free and easy access to the throne of grace now had to depend on the atonement by the blood of animals to obtain mercy from the Almighty.

In spite of all this the atonement by the blood of animals was just too inadequate to restore him back to the place of heavenly bliss and intimate communion he once knew. It only brought man a seasonal relief that was unsatisfactory. Occasionally, by the infinite mercies of the Lord, a few persons were visited and so granted the privilege to walk under open heavens for a brief moment. Such individuals were then given a glimpse into the life that was meant to be our normal everyday experience.

By such repeated visitations, a few were able to escape the adverse effect of the spiritual drought. Like the migrating animals, their determination to walk away from death into life motivated them, and the great journey to the Promised Land began.

He who was meant to live life in a glorious paradise on earth became a pilgrim and a stranger in the domain where he was born a king and priest.

Abraham, Isaac, and Jacob had glimpses of it. Moses died trying to bring the children of Israel into the shadow of this substance. David became so dissatisfied with the occasional trickles he received from the presence of God that he was moved to cry out, "O God, you are my God, earnestly I seek you; my soul thirsts for you, my body longs for you, like a dry and weary land where there is no water."[2]

These men could sense there was much more to what they were experiencing, but there was no way they could gain access into it. Just when they thought it was within reach, it suddenly faded away like a mirage.

They all in anticipation hungered and thirsted for it but were unable to see it fulfilled in their days. The prophet Joel rejoiced to see the light at the end of the tunnel; being lifted in the Spirit he heard the Lord say, "And afterward, I will pour out my Spirit on all people. Your sons and daughters will prophesy. Your young men will dream dreams, even on my servants, both men and women, I will pour out my Spirit in those days."[3]

This was the greatest news of them all. At last, the day would come when the soul of man could rest from wandering. This silver lining became an impetus for a fresh longing and anticipation for the actual manifestation of the promise. It was the gathering of the clouds which brought some hope that the end of this spiritual drought was in sight.

Though this promise was not made manifest until many years later, in the fullness of time God sent His Son to offer a once-for-all atonement which restored man to the place of fellowship with the Father (Ephesians 1:3-14 and Galatians 4:4-5).

After this was accomplished, Jesus came to His disciples to announce to them the good news.

> He told them, this is what is written; the Christ will suffer and rise from the dead on the third day, and repentance and forgiveness of sins will be preached in his name to all nations, beginning at Jerusalem. You are witnesses of these things. I am going to send you what my Father has promised; but stay in the city until you have been clothed with power from on high.[4]

Only a few days earlier they were the most miserable folks on earth, but now they were about to see the fulfillment of what many great prophets had hoped for. In a matter of days they would be clothed with the very power of God as His precious Holy Spirit came to dwell in their own spirits. And they did experience it.

It was the dawn of a new beginning. The atonement of Christ had opened for all who believed an access to the very presence of God, and the soul of man could now rest from wandering. Finally the anticipation was over and His will could be done on earth as it is in heaven. Hallelujah!

Sparse or Abundant Release

The manifestation of the presence of God in most worship experiences today is scarce or in some cases very irregular.

In some assemblies, the manifestation of the presence of God has been limited to annual revivals and conventions. The people are no longer certain of the visitation of God during the regular weekly worship service, and worship has become more of a routine than an encounter with the living God. When people come in hungry and thirsty, they repeatedly have their expectation dashed, and one cannot help but ask: what is wrong?

The Lord said,

> I withheld rain from you when the harvest was still three months away. I sent rain on one town but withheld it from another. One field had rain; and another had none and dried up. People staggered from town to town for water but did not get enough to drink, yet you have not returned to me, declares the LORD.[5]

Irregular manifestation of the presence of God in our worship is often an indication there is a problem in our relationship with God. Sometimes the problem is that we take it for granted that God will always show up as long as we are doing something in His name. This is a big error. God does not just endorse anything that has His name attached to it.

If we fail to seek His face for His leading or fail to follow divine instructions on how to go about our worship, He will not bless our meetings with His awesome presence.

Before the disciples could experience the release of the promise of the Father, they were obedient to the instruction of the Lord to go to Jerusalem and wait till they were endued with power from on high. They obeyed simple instructions. God will not bless us with His presence if we are not committed to seek and do His will by following simple instructions.

The release of rain from heaven has always been in response to an action from the earth. From my little knowledge of science, it is said that the formation of clouds has to do with the collection of water vapor from a particular area. When this vapor rises, it will solidify to form cloud and then fall back as rain. It is then reasonable to say "what you give is what you get." If nothing is given, nothing should be expected.

Those in the dry and arid regions of the earth experience scanty rain because the atmosphere above them has received little or nothing from the land. Therefore, the land is said to be scorched and barren. But those of us who live in the rainforest region of the earth can have the blessing of rain all through the year because there is more than enough condensation taking place. The sky is always cloudy and the vegetation of the land is always green.

When God promised to take His children to the Promised Land, the land was described as "...a land with streams and pools of water, with springs flowing in the valleys and hills...."[6] Therefore, this land has the guarantee of abundant rain and vibrant life.

Those who are always thirsty for more of God will always occupy the Promised Land with abundant water supply. Those who know how to saturate heaven with their worship will never lack the release of heaven's rain.

When we fail to saturate heaven with our worship we will lack the all important blessing of the rain we need to help make our harvest rich and abundant.

This is the word of the Lord to His people through the prophet Amos in the passage we referred to earlier in Amos 4:7-8. If we start in the Spirit and then choose to do our own thing, we will hinder the release of the latter rain that will help determine the quality and quantity of our harvest.

But for those who stay in constant communion with the Lord through it all, the Lord has promised to bless them with the latter and the former rain (Deuteronomy 11:14, Hosea 6:3, Joel 2:23).

When the disciples gathered together with one passion waiting for the promise of the Father, their prayers ascended to heaven and in no time there was a release from heaven that was described as the sound of a mighty rushing wind (Acts 2:2). Those of us who live in the rainforest can tell how heavy the rain will be just by observing the wind and the clouds.

If we must see the release of rain upon our parched lands, then we must make an effort to bring together thirsty souls who are hungry for more of God. As we worship God with one passion, the heavens will be moved to release the rain of God's presence over our land.

Preachers like Billy Graham, Benny Hinn, and Reinhard Bonnke are able to record extraordinary miracles in their meetings because they know how to assemble a team made up of those who are passionate for God. In Africa, one of the reasons preachers are able to record unusual miracles is because those who come to these meetings come with a lot of expectations and hunger for God. They know that except God show up there is no hope. They don't have the sophisticated technology that people in the Western world look up to, so when they come to these meetings their faith is in God. As they worship with great passion and expectation, you can sense their faith rising and suddenly heaven is moved to respond to their hunger, and mighty miracles, signs, and wonders begin to happen all over the ground as many are saved, healed, and delivered.

If we will teach the various units or ministering groups of our churches to become hungry and thirsty for the visitation of God in our meetings, when we gather it will be with one passion, and as our faith rises to heaven the clouds will begin to gather and in no time there will be a heavy downpour of heaven's rain. Through the prophet Isaiah, we can see that the Lord responds to passionate and thirsty souls. He has said,

> When the poor and needy search for water and there is none, and their tongues are parched from thirst, then I, the LORD, will answer them. I, the God of Israel, will never forsake them. I will open up rivers for them on high plateaus. I will give them fountains of water in the valleys. In the desert they will find pools of water. Rivers fed by springs will flow across the dry, parched ground.[7]

When the rain begins to fall from heaven, the atmosphere will suddenly change, and as people are soaked in this rain the flood of blessings, healings, and all kinds of miracles will sweep over our souls.

Our Preparation Is Vital

You can tell how important a person or group is by the level of preparation undertaken for their visit. In some cases such personalities or events may not come to the city if it is believed that the city has not met the requirement to host such dignitaries or events. A very good example is the hosting of big sporting events like the FIFA soccer World Cup and the Olympic Games. The hosting right of competitions of this magnitude is always given to a city that is considered to be the best prepared. That notwithstanding, after the hosting right has been awarded to a city or country, a special committee is appointed to monitor the level of preparation of the host city or country. It is only when the various requirements have been met that the city is able to host the event.

It is amazing that many of us in the church understand and appreciate the need for such elaborate preparation to host a sporting event but are very nonchalant about our preparation to host the Creator of the universe in our worship, and then we expect Him to show up. Why should He show up when we do not take Him seriously? Don't you think He has better things to do and more serious places to go?

If we fail to reverently prepare to host Him we will pay dearly for it. When Eli the high priest of Israel failed to make his children revere God and by so doing caused the people to sin against God, the Lord sent a prophet to tell him this sad message:

> "...I promised that your house and your father's house would minister before me forever, but now the LORD declares: 'Far be it from me! Those who honor me I will honor, but those who despise me will be disdained.'"[8]

God walked away from Eli's ministry because he failed to honor God, and in addition to this he suffered so many calamities in just one day that he fell backwards from his chair and died (1 Samuel 4:10-18).

God has walked away from many lives and religious gatherings because we have not learnt to honor Him. If we honor Him, He will honor our meetings with His presence.

The Wilderness Worship

Today most worship has become the display of the superiority of intellect, doctrine, and traditions which are so irrelevant to the true thirst and hunger of souls who are desperate to encounter God. This is a far cry from the prophetic declaration of the prophet Joel and the undeniable presence of God evident in the apostles' ministry as recorded in the Acts of the Apostles.

So many houses of worship tell people, "This is the place to be," but they have nothing tangible to show for it. They go by all sorts of wonderful and catchy names, promising heaven on earth, but unfortunately, no sooner than people make their way there in great expectation do they discover it is all dry and empty. Their expectation was raised only for them to find there is no hope in this place for their weary souls. There is a drought in this land. The cloud that releases the rain of His presence in worship is nowhere to be found.

They have sat down meeting after meeting and nothing glorious happened. Slowly and steadily they became uncomfortable in this drought. So, in one more desperate effort to survive, they head for the door hoping to find the Promised Land before it is too late.

Jesus knew there was no way the disciples could make any lasting impact without the power of the Holy Spirit, so He told them to go and wait for the heavenly visitation.

If pastors and worship leaders will wait long enough to be empowered from above, our worship experience will become a glorious and life-changing experience. People long to be in a place where the cloud of worship freely and easily releases on them the refreshing rain of God's presence. They will not mind traveling a long distance just to bask in God's presence.

The promise given to Joel and made manifest in the time of the apostles can still be a very active part of our worship today if we will take time to seek the Lord. We don't have to go on wandering in the wilderness. There is a way to end this drought.

From Wilderness to Wonderland

> When the day of Pentecost came, suddenly a sound like the blowing of a violent wind came from heaven and filled the whole house where they were sitting. They saw what seemed to be tongues of fire that separated and came to rest on each of them. All of them were filled with the Holy Spirit and began to speak in other tongues as the Spirit enabled them.[9]

Without the enabling power of the Holy Spirit, the disciples of Jesus would have become irrelevant in their time. In themselves they lacked the pedigree to stand the powerful religious leaders of their day who were ready to eliminate any threat to their traditions.

They needed something more than mere argument and religious zeal. It had to be something supernatural, and it came through the Pentecost experience.

The difference was phenomenal. It was unbelievable. From the time of the arrest of Jesus up until Pentecost, there had not been one occasion where they boldly made mention of the name of Jesus in public. There is no record of any public worship activity among them. They became too scared to speak of the Lord. But once they were empowered from above by the Holy Spirit, they began to worship with such passion and noise that it attracted the attention of people all over Jerusalem. With boldness they began to speak about Jesus in such a passionate way that the people were moved to ask, "What shall we do?"[10]

This happened because the rain that was released from heaven upon them had become a flood that overwhelmed and softened the parched heart of those who came to see what was happening. Whenever our worship is empowered by the person of the Holy Spirit, it will leave men with the willingness to come close to God.

You will not need to manipulate the emotions of people; they will suddenly become willing and ready to do anything. They have been taken right in their hearts, and at this point they just need a guide.

Showers of Refreshing

When Peter was through with his message on the day of Pentecost, about three thousand souls were added to the church (Acts 2:41). Can you imagine what this will do to some of our churches that have been struggling to grow for some years now?

In search of the solution, some have attended church growth conferences and seminars. They have applied different methods and steps, but nothing extraordinary happened. All they truly need is the presence of the Holy Spirit and the difference will be clear. If people can see that what we have will bring refreshing to their souls, they will become willing to drink from the river that has risen from the rain from above.

When Peter and John prayed for the lame man at the temple gate called Beautiful and he was healed, they immediately got the attention of the people. It is recorded that the people actually ran to them in great wonder (Acts 3:11). The people saw that what the apostles had was beyond mere words. It became obvious that they had more than religion. Peter was able to use this opportunity to stir up their hunger for more of God. He called them to repentance with the promise of a refreshing that would visit them from the presence of the Lord, and five thousand souls were saved.

Some years back when we started the BSF group, we were less than twenty people. One day as we spent time seeking the face of the Lord, I heard Him say, "Behold the few that will bring forth the multitude." And in less than a year we had a growth explosion.

You don't need a crowd to shake your city. All you need is the rain of His presence and the spiritually famished will locate you. They will come from the north, south, east, and west to refresh their weary souls. You will not have to struggle to keep them; they will be only too glad to be part of where God is at work to refresh their souls.

As they are refreshed by the rain from God's presence they will become passionate to be more like the Lord as they are transformed in this Spirit-filled worship.

As the psalmist observed, people become willing when they see the manifestation of the supernatural (Psalm 110:3). They will begin to grow in intimacy with the Lord. Those you thought would never amount to anything will suddenly amaze all who have known them prior to that visitation.

Men cannot help but wonder when heaven in travail brings forth her children.

If we will sincerely follow the true longing of our souls, we will reach the place where many souls will come running just to encounter the refreshing from the presence of the Lord in our worship. It is the showers of refreshing.

God has never left us without a place to refresh our souls. This is the reason He gave the children of Israel a clear picture of the land He was taking them to as they came out of Egypt to go to the Promised Land. He said through His servant Moses, "...the Lord your God is bringing you into a good land—a land with streams and pools of water, with springs flowing in the valleys and hills."[11]

God has already provided a way to refresh the souls of men, but until we are able to find it we cannot lead others there. If you can't find it, they will try somewhere else. But if you do find it, you will be amazed at the results that follow. If you seek for it with all your heart, it will be yours. The cloud above us is the one we have created by the kind of worship we offer unto God. If we will give Him quality worship He will cause the heavens to open and pour upon our land the rain of His presence. He has said, "Call to me and I will answer you and tell you great and unsearchable things you do not know."[12]

CHAPTER ELEVEN

THE SEASON OF GREAT OUTPOURING

> Who has heard such a thing?
> Who has seen such a thing?
> Can a land be born in one day?
> Can a nation be brought forth all at once?
> As soon as Zion travailed, she also brought forth her sons.[1]

The days of drought among God's people are gradually coming to an end. The Lord Himself is stirring up His people to the place where there will be another great revival in the church.

By reason of the drought which has been in the church for a long time now, God's people are groaning in a growing discontent leading to a cry for divine intervention. The church is in travail. Zion is about to bring forth her sons in the most unusual way. In some places, it will have been a concluded issue before many will know it. The delivery will be like nothing we have heard or seen before. For as soon as Zion travails, she will bring forth. This will happen so fast for a number of reasons.

1. By reason of the drought which has prevailed over the church for so long, many have lost the vision they were once so passionate about, but right now the eyes of many have been opened to the despair and degradation of the church, and many are in travail crying for the restoration of the glory.

2. The darkness is increasing its effort to overwhelm the souls of men all over the world with new strategies. Wickedness and satanic opinions are gaining acceptance and recognition in their repackaged forms. And they seem to be effective in their scheme to enslave the souls of men like never before. Fear, depression, frustration, and death are on the prowl to waste precious souls.

The forces of spiritual darkness are mercilessly attacking infants and youths to gain control of the future by building in their minds a strong resentment against God and intolerance for godly principles. They are using all kinds of intimidation and molestation against the older generation by labeling them as narrow-minded and intolerant folks.

But our God has an answer in advance. Another great move of the Spirit that will erupt like a tsunami is coming. We are about to see the glory of the Lord overshadow the church and the entire world like never before (Isaiah 60:1).

This revival will bring about a revolution that will help redefine culture and concepts. As people are taken by this revival, they will begin to burn with great excitement, and in no time they will invade the culture of this world with the culture of the kingdom of God.

3. Time is running out. Time they say waits for no man, and "what you have to do, do it quickly." There is so much to be done, and the Lord who is all-knowing and all-wise knows just what to do to redeem the time. Currently, the Lord is using strange and unconventional ways to redeem the time. He is doing so because most individuals and churches have failed Him by their rigid attachment to their protocol, bureaucracy, legalism, traditions, and doctrines.

As in the parable of the great banquet told by Jesus in Luke 14, because so many of us claim to be too busy to respond to the call of the Lord, He is enlisting men from the highway and byway. They may not have gone through any theological institution or religious system, yet they possess great insight of the Scriptures coupled with an undaunted faith that is affirmed by signs and wonders. Unconventional and unusual worshippers will become the catalyst by which the process is accelerated. As they travail in worship, the presence of the Lord will be released and many will be endued with power from on high. This revival is here.

The Ozoro Outpouring

In the process of writing this book, I accepted an invitation to be the camp pastor for a teen camp meeting held from August 30 to September 3, 2007, at a place called Ozoro in Delta state Nigeria. As I spent time in prayer seeking the face of the Lord, I heard these words in my spirit: "The great outpouring." I quickly wrote this down, thinking it was the topic for one of the messages during the camp, but as the Lord spoke to me I was able to see that this had to do with the move of God that we were about to experience in this camp meeting. The Lord further said, "Many of them (teens) are coming to this camp as unfinished works that must be attended to." Suddenly my spirit was stirred with an unusual burden, accompanied by an awareness of the urgency of the task ahead of me.

Right from our takeoff point in the city of Warri, I saw that some of these teenagers were stubborn and disrespectful. Others were either ignorant or proudly living on Fantasy Island. But a few were hungry for a touch from the Lord. I knew it was not going to be an easy task with this mixed multitude, so I asked the Lord for some strange manifestations.

The message of the first night and that of the second day was more of a groundbreaking experience. By the third day, 90 percent of them had become more open to the Lord as a great number of teens responded to the call to give their lives to God. At the close of the third day, they were sober and focused.

They had been bombarded by the Word preached through various speakers.

When Sunday morning came, I knew it was time to stir up their hunger for more of the presence of God, because the Lord had laid it on my heart to challenge them with this word: "Let the world see His glory." At first it took some effort to get their full attention as we all had not had breakfast, and you can imagine what that means to teenagers. But as I began to share about the great outpouring, the Spirit of the Lord took over and there was this unusual hush. I could tell they were now hungry for God and full of expectation. The majority of them were stunned by the prophecy of Joel I had spoken on. There was no time for doubts to prevail because as we started worshipping the Lord in songs, the power of God came down and people fell under the power of the Holy Spirit all over the hall without anyone laying hands on them.

By the time the service was over, everyone knew something glorious had begun. It was now lunchtime but nobody cared. I stayed on after the service to counsel and pray with some who saw the need to share the issues of their heart with me. During this session, one of the girls in confidence shared with me her bitter experience of sexual molestation from the age of five and the series of satanic attacks she had experienced for over ten years. She spoke sobbing and wondering if things would ever be different. The Lord filled my heart with compassion, and I felt His presence all over. I led her in prayers to reject the dominion of the power of darkness and to rededicate her life to the Lord. As she did, the power of God came on her, and she was on the floor screaming.

Soon after the screaming stopped, I sensed God's leading to pray asking the Holy Spirit to fill her with His presence. Within seconds, the power and presence of God took over and she began to prophesy. I asked the brother assisting me to write down the prophecy so I could check it out to be sure it was in line with Scripture. I was overwhelmed by what I discovered, and this was only the beginning.

God was really at work beyond my imagination. Two others, a boy and a girl, said their eyes were opened to see the Lord during the meeting. I had no doubt something unusual was happening. By the time I was through with them, it was already about 3:30 p.m. I had a short time to eat and rest before the evening session, but somehow I knew the Lord was not through with these teenagers. I could sense the glorious presence and power of God all over the campground. But it occurred to me that if they stuck to the program lined up for the camp, then the evening session would be a campfire celebration time, and I was certain the power would fall there too and it would not be easy to manage.

Just when I was contemplating what to do, the coordinator of the camp, Deacon J. Eni, came to say there would not be a campfire. He said he sensed that God was not through and that two of the teenagers told him the Lord spoke to them that He was not through. It was so amazing the way the confirmations came. A great revival had begun.

When we gathered that Sunday evening, everyone came with some expectation and the presence of God became so tangible in the hall during the praise and worship. As the singers handed the microphone to me, the presence of the Lord was so strong I could not open my Bible. I wanted to sing a song, but before I could say the first word of the song the glory fell and one of the girls was completely overwhelmed by the Holy Spirit and began to prophesy. Suddenly she dashed into the crowd and got hold of somebody and bought her to me as she gave a word of knowledge of this person's situation. I then laid hands on this other girl and she went down under the power. Before I was through, she was back with another and another and another person, and the Lord came upon all of them.

Some of them were so filled with the Spirit they began to lay hands on others who were also filled with the Spirit until the whole place was charged with the power of God.

There were diverse manifestations. Demons cried out as some were set free and the glory of the Lord took over. Some

were crying as they repented of their sins while others prophesied or spoke in tongues.

It became so awesome that at a point I just stood there
in amazement, giving glory to God. This was truly awesome,
beyond what I have been able to narrate here. I found a way to
officially close the service about 3:30 a.m. (Monday morning),
yet these teenagers were so awestruck they found it difficult
to step out of the auditorium. They were gripped with reverential fear as they watched others around them still basking
in the presence of God. Some were so drunk in the Spirit they
could not walk. We prayed asking God to strengthen them.
Only then were they able to walk to their hostel with some
support.

When the coordinator came to the room, he came back
with shoes and a bag he picked up on the way. They were items
abandoned by those who were so drunk in the Spirit.

As we reflected on all that had just happened, we agreed
that we had never seen the power of God move this way before,
and my mind went to the dedication of Solomon's temple when
the presence of God fell and the priests could not minister.

I am eternally grateful to God for giving me the opportunity to be a part of this great encounter.

After only a little sleep, I was outside brushing my teeth
when somebody came to inform me that two of the girls were
still prophesying in their hostel. I went back into the room and
sent somebody to go see to it. Then it became obvious to us
that it is not going to be easy to conduct the closing session
that morning. The hired buses were already around to convey
people back, and we could not afford to pay anything extra,
so we decided not to preach, sing, or do anything that would
stir up the atmosphere. This was the kind of revival and outpouring that could have gone from days into weeks if we had
the time and resources, but because we were so far from home
and had little resources, we asked God to help us close the
meeting and we succeeded.

But right in the thirty-seat bus that I boarded, I heard this
unusual screaming. The power of God fell on a girl in the back

seat, and she went off in tongues. Everyone in the bus was amazed. I later gathered that the same thing happened in one other bus and that they had to support some of them home.

Can you imagine their parents opening the door to see their sons and daughters staggering into the house? They would have been too amazed to find out that they were not under the influence of alcohol or drugs but under the power of the Holy Spirit. The revival is here.

The Birth of a Great Revival

When I got home to my family that Monday, I could not help but reflect on the event of the past few days. In amazement I could not help but wonder what would follow. Without doubt I knew things could never be the same again. God had taken over and something had begun that would prepare the next generation for a mighty move of God.

This whole thing was just a taste of what is to come.

Early Tuesday morning I got a call from the brother of one of the girls sounding apprehensive. He told me that two of the girls could not stop prophesying. It was so strong they could not even get them to eat. I was asked to come over to help calm them down. But by the time I got there, I met this brother outside the house waiting for me. He said there was a new development since his last call; the girls in their drunken state had gone to the end of the street. And when I got to the house where they were, they were prophesying over two young guys, who were on their knees asking God for mercy as they gave their hearts to the Lord.

Immediately after, the two girls got a leading to go lead a girl to the Lord some six streets away, and they went on foot under the rain. I offered to take them there in my car, but they chose to walk. By the time they got there, they stormed the house of this girl in a manner that got her brother and mother apprehensive and on the defensive. But when they understood that the girls came with a message from the Lord, they opened up and in no time the girl was on her knees dedicating her life to God.

The method was so unconventional and strange, but it was producing quick and unusual results to the glory of God.

After this particular encounter, I was able to get them to go with me to the church. And that became the beginning of a training process for them.

A Divine Visitation

News about the move of the Lord got to the leadership of this Baptist church, and I was invited to come lead the prayer service that Wednesday morning. In the course of the meeting, the power and presence of the Lord took over and the girls were again overwhelmed by the power of God. The whole place became charged with the presence of the Lord and many gave their lives to God. Others were filled with the Spirit as hands were laid on them.

A week after the teenagers' camp meeting people were still being filled with fresh fire from heaven. Many lives were restored to the place of fellowship with God, and God became so real and the Scriptures a living reality.

A revival fire had been kindled in families, and the church and the community were being transformed. Obviously, this was a visitation of God upon His people. The lost were saved, the sick were healed, and the demon-possessed were set free. The worship experience of many was transformed from just another event to a time of divine visitation.

It was the dawn of a new beginning, and I feel honored to have seen the manifestation of the power of God in this magnitude. Now I understood what Benny Hinn meant when he would say, "I wonder if it is going to happen again." But I think it will. I may not know exactly when or how, but I can sense God is not through. Why? Our generation is yet to experience anything close to the Charles Finney kind of revival in which a whole city was saved by the move of God with an impact that continued for years. In such cities, the people lived in conscious reality of the presence of God. So powerful was the revival that miles and miles away from the place of meeting people got convicted of their sins and surrendered their lives to God. Worship here was not just a religious activity. It was the response of the hearts of men to the prompting of God.

I used to read of the visitation of God in books, but now I believe I have had a glimpse into this glorious manifestation, and there must be more for a generation like ours that has been invaded by all kinds of delusion, deception, and corruption.

Heaven knows we need a wave of God's revival to restore the church back to the place of passionate worship, and the time is now.

If the glory of the latter will be greater than that of the former, then there must be something more than what we have ever seen or heard.

There is a shift in the heavens, and Zion is in travail to give birth to the next generation of God's generals that will storm the world in the most unusual fashion.

It will look strange in the eyes of the traditional and religious bunch, but it will be authenticated with unusual signs and manifestations that cannot be ignored. What we need is not the old-time religion but the old-time revival that is often characterized by such awesome awakening that it grips the heart and causes hardened criminals to fall in reverence of God.

Most of what has been named revival recently is a far cry from what should be called revival. If it was a revival, it would stir the hearts of men to worship.

When the prophet Elijah called down fire from heaven in 1 Kings 18, the people saw it and immediately fell on their faces and worshipped, crying, "The LORD—he is God! The LORD—he is God!"[2] Any religious experience that is not capable of causing men to fall down to worship in reverential awe is not qualified to be called a revival.

That which motivates men to seek their own materialistic gain is not the revival we speak of. It may have drawn both the high and mighty to your meetings, but until it causes them to bow in worship and produces the transformation of their lives, it was not the revival we speak of. When there is a revival in the land, the kings and nobles of the land will not hesitate to bow in worship. They will be too willing to lay aside the pomp and pageantry that go with their office to acknowledge the presence of the King of Kings.

Certainly the day is at hand when in our generation we will see again the great revival that shakes cities and nations, stirring in men a fresh passion to worship. It will happen suddenly in the most unusual ways, and some of it may be stirred up by events that are not very pleasant, but at the end it will lead the hearts of men to seek the Lord like never before. The great revival is here.

Stay connected to God and the eyes of your understanding will be enlightened to see and follow the move of the Holy Spirit.

The man who is spiritual is the man who has trained his senses to recognize and follow the move of the Spirit. These are the army of the Lord prophesied about by Joel in Joel 2. Are you a part of this army?

CHAPTER TWELVE

ENTERING THE GLORY
OF HIS PRESENCE

There are realms of glory we may never walk in until we learn some of the secrets of the way of the Spirit. There is a path designed to usher us from one degree of glory to another.

The further you travel on this road, the greater will be the manifestation of God's glory upon your life. The closer you are to the Lord, the more sensitive you become to locate the way.

The prophet Moses was privileged to encounter the awesome glory of God because his first desire was to become intimate with God. While communing with the Lord, he said, "If you are pleased with me, **teach me your ways** so I may know you and continue to find favor with you...."[1]

Many want to record the success that goes with the glory without a genuine hunger to please God and a readiness to pay the price. If you are not intimate with Him you cannot know Him. If you don't know Him you cannot walk in His glory.

To know Him is to become acquainted with the passion of His heart. It is a determination to gain insight into the feelings of His heart. It is a drive to know and to do that which is well pleasing in His sight.

If we seek to please Him, He will begin to disclose to us the feelings of His heart, and only then will we be able to see and understand His ways. When we begin to perceive His ways, we will become intimate with Him and our hearts will overflow with a burning passion to do His will.

At this point it will please Him to usher us into realms of glory that will enable us to do far beyond our abilities.

Those who are continually favored with the glory of His presence have learnt to stay their feet on the path of righteousness.

If we cannot take time to understand His ways we cannot enter into deeper realms of His glory. The Word of God tells us that His ways are past finding out. They are untraceable (Romans 11:33). You cannot discover it. It is only revealed by the Spirit.

The Passion and the Glory

He who seeks acquaintance with God has chosen the path of ever increasing glory. This is my personal submission and testimony. After I gave my life to Christ, I sought for and craved for more acquaintance with God, and I began to encounter God. As I spent time in prayer, reading the Bible, and soaking up the ministries of anointed preachers, I became more aware of the life in the Spirit and began to notice some glorious manifestations. My spiritual eyes were opened and I began to see things. At first they were just flashes of a few seconds that were not too explicit, but later it became more detailed visions and dreams. My ears were opened and I began to hear and commune with the Holy Spirit, and it became an intimate walk which He confirmed with answers to prayers as I lay on hands praying for the healing of the sick and afflicted.

The more results I got the more people and stress that came with it. It then occurred to me that it would be better to have the Lord touch the people than for me to wear myself out trying to pray for several sick and afflicted people in a large meeting. Besides, He alone knows the history of those present and how best to meet their needs. So I cried out to God for help and He heard my cry. This was when the gift of the word of knowledge became more prominent. It is fascinating and lovely to see the Lord confirm His word as I call out the needs of people under His leading. Just to see them healed, delivered, saved, and filled with the presence and power of God without touching anyone is truly amazing. Most of the time it is hard to comprehend. In such moments, I cannot help but thank Him for choosing to use me to bring glory to His name because I know that of myself I am not worthy of this honor. In such moments of glory I have come to see that there is nothing, absolutely nothing, impossible with God.

During our 2009 Easter worship experience tagged "The Passion and the Glory," we saw a degree of the manifestation of God's glory like we had never seen it before. When the glory was revealed, many began to cry out to God as they were saved, delivered, and filled with the Holy Spirit.

We saw every sick person who came forward healed. The glory was so great that even a lady who didn't believe the healing would happen to her was healed on the spot. It happened just after she came forward wondering if what was occurring in the meeting was real. The Lord led me to say to her that the pain down her spine was moving up her neck, and she in amazement confirmed it to be true. Then the Lord said "it is leaving" and she began to rejoice as she confirmed that it was true, and that was how she got her healing. As we all watched this happening, it stirred in us a greater sense of awe and reverence for God, fueling our passion to worship the King of Glory.

That was a wonderful experience, and how I wish all our meetings ended like this. If you have ever led a meeting or prayed believing for the healing or deliverance of people only to see them leave with little or no evidential change, you will understand what I mean. There are times when I wonder why the Lord did not do it for some, and then I begin to wonder if I and all in the team have been sensitive and obedient enough to let God have His way to manifest Himself in that meeting. Sometimes I feel if we had been more sensitive, we would have seen or heard more about the will of God for that meeting. We all have an important role to play as we partner with God to see His glory manifest in our worship.

That notwithstanding, God is sovereign and can do anything, any way He pleases. Sometimes it is not the degree of our readiness; He just decided to glorify His name. If we will sincerely follow after Him, He will open unto us greater and deeper realms of glory.

It was after Moses got the guarantee from the Lord that His presence would go with him (acquaintance) that he was able to say, "Now show me your glory."[2]

If you miss the way you cannot find the glory. Actually, if your heart is passionate for God you cannot miss the way. The heart that is passionate for Him is one that is being driven by a hunger to know Him in spirit and in truth; therefore this person cannot miss it. Just before this soul misses the way the Lord has promised to put him back on track:

> Whether you turn to the right or to the left,
> your ears will hear a voice behind you, saying,
> "This is the way; walk in it."[3]

We can find the way and stay our feet on the path of glory if we will sincerely ask the Lord to help us. If we fail to acknowledge our inadequacies we will miss it.

Some time ago, as I communed with the Lord in my time of personal worship, I was inspired to speak words which later became the text of a song titled "New Degrees of Glory." This is the content of that communion with God as it flowed out of my spirit:

As we walk in the Spirit all day.
As we walk through the bright path of glory,
We express life in the Spirit and manifest your power.
May there be new degrees of glory.

May there be new degrees of glory.
A higher height of glory in the Spirit.
May there be new degrees of glory.
A higher height of glory in the Lord.[4]

There is more to our walk with the Lord. Just a glimpse into the glory the Father desires for us to walk in and we will be too ashamed of what we call "awesome" or "glorious."

The Father's desire is to set before us an open door that will usher us into a realm of ever increasing glory, but many of us are not sensitive enough to see this. The further you travel on this road, the greater the glory He bestows. It all depends on how far you are willing to go.

Passion, Purpose, and Splendor

Many who seek to carry the glorious presence of the Lord are too insensitive to the heartbeat of the Lord. They are often more passionate about their own agenda than they are about the purpose of the Lord.

If the Lord cannot trust you with the secrets of His heart there will be no need to trust you with the glory. To know the splendor of His majesty is to become dedicated to His purpose. The realm of glory belongs to those who take pleasure in pleasing the Lord.

Moses saw the glory of the Lord because he cared about the Father's desire to bring the children of Israel to the Promised Land as a nation wholly devoted to Yahweh. Once Moses knew the heart desires of the Lord, it became his passion, purpose, and pursuit. All other things became secondary.

This is the reason why his first request was a desire to know the way, and once he knew the way it became appropriate to know the glory.

Those who seek accolades for themselves have no business in this realm of glory before God. Those who seek for prestige or glamour may succeed in fooling mortals but not the immortal and all-knowing God. The man who craves after and delights in a divine fellowship with Him who dwells in light inaccessible will become flooded with light and can never be obscured or irrelevant.

The soul that seeks to do the will of the Father will graciously progress from one degree of glory to another. As glorious doors are opened unto them, things beyond their wildest dream will manifest.

Once you have come to know the blessing of His presence, nothing else will do. You will not want anything to interfere with your heart-to-heart communion with the Lord. This is the passion we find expressed in the song "To Keep Your Lovely Face" by Bob Fitts and the Maranatha! Singers. It says,

> To keep Your lovely face, ever before my eyes,
> This is my prayer, make it my soul desire.
> That in my secret heart, no other love competes
> No rival throne survives and I serve only you.[5]

A careful study of this lyric reveals that this is a pledge of total allegiance to the lover of our souls. It is an expression of a determination to maintain zero tolerance for any rival throne.

What is a rival throne? A rival throne is anything that is able to delay your positive response to the Lord. If you must do its bidding before you do that of the Lord, it is a rival throne.

Whatsoever is strong enough to determine where you go and how much time you spend in worship is a rival throne. If it is able to steal your attention away from the Lord in your moment of worship, it is a rival throne. If you find pleasure in it more than in the worship of God, it is a rival throne.

The soul that is sold out to God has very little patience for anything that competes for the place of the Lord in his or her heart. There is no secret agenda with this soul when it stands in worship. The Lord rules and reigns here undisputable.

We are only able to dwell in the secret place when the Lord rules and reigns in our secret heart.

To this soul, every moment of worship is a precious opportunity to bask in the avalanche of love that flows from the throne of grace. It is another opportunity to experience the mighty surge of God's presence and power and a privilege to be a witness for Him. This is the joy and pleasure of this soul passionate after God.

The Unfolding of a More Excellent Glory

In the book of Exodus, the Lord gave the prophet Moses the rare privilege of not only standing in His presence but also the honor of seeing His back form. As Moses communed with God he did not know he was being transformed by the glory of God (Exodus 34:8). When he came down from Mount Sinai, Aaron and all the people saw this unusual glow from his face, and they could tell it was the glory of God and became afraid to go close. It was then Moses realized the degree of transformation that had taken place while he communed with the Lord.

There is a realm of glory greater than what you carry right now, but it will only unfold as you sincerely seek the Lord.

In the days of Moses, he was the only one who had the privilege to gain access into God's glorious presence, but today we all can enter in. The personality and precious gift of the Holy Spirit has made it available and accessible to all (Ephesians 2:13-18).

If we are willing, we will walk in and manifest a glory greater than what Moses had. When Paul wrote to the Corinthian church, he wanted them to see that this is possible for those redeemed by the blood of Christ, in whom the Spirit lives and moves. He said,

> Now if the ministry that brought death, which was engraved in letters on stone, came with glory, so that the Israelites could not look steadily at the face of Moses because of its glory, fading though it was, will not the ministry of the Spirit be even more glorious? If the ministry that condemns men is glorious, how much more glorious is the ministry that brings righteousness, for what was glorious has no

glory now in comparison with the surpassing glory.[6]

Ours is a glory that does not fade like that of Moses. It is a glory that enables us to bring the Spirit of life to those we come in contact with, but the law Moses had ministered death.

What the apostle Paul had ministered life, and by it God preformed unusual miracles. Handkerchiefs or aprons that had contact with Paul were placed on the sick and they were all healed; those possessed with evil spirits were set free (Acts 19:11).

When people recognized this glory on the apostle Peter, they "...brought the sick into the streets and laid them on beds and mats so that at least Peter's shadow might fall on some of them as he passed by. Crowds gathered also from the towns around Jerusalem, bringing their sick and those tormented by evil spirits, and all of them were healed."[7] What a glory! This can be our testimony if we will only allow the Spirit of the Lord to have His way in our lives.

> Now the Lord is the Spirit, and where the Spirit of the Lord is, there is freedom. And we, who with unveiled faces all reflect the Lord's glory, are being transformed into his likeness with ever-increasing glory, which comes from the Lord, who is the Spirit.[8]

The River of Glory

A careful study of the Bible reveals that most of the prophets of old experienced an unusual lift in their ministry when they encountered the glory of the Father. After they entered this realm of glory, their testimony became more of "He showed me," "I heard a voice," "He brought me to," and the like.

When the Father sees the content of a heart, He knows just when to take that soul to the next level of divine encounter. Nobody thought the young shepherd and musician of

Bethlehem had the qualification to serve in the king's court, but right before the eyes of his father and siblings he was anointed king of Israel.

In Ezekiel 40, the hand of the Lord came upon the prophet Ezekiel when he was among other captives in Babylon, and he was taken into the realm of the Spirit. As others continued their weeping by the river of Babylon, right there he was taken in his spirit to access the realm of glory. From such an encounter, he received divine enablement by the help of a heavenly being, who said to him,

> ...Son of man, look with your eyes and hear with your ears and pay attention to everything I am going to show you, for that is why you have been brought here. Tell the house of Israel everything you see.[9]

When our heart is prepared for a new realm of glory, it will become sensitive to both hear and see things by the instrumentality of the Holy Spirit. The prerequisite to access the realms of the Spirit is not the aspiration in the heart of a man but the condition and passion of that heart.

The realms of the Spirit we walk in are of different degrees. In Ezekiel 47, God gave the prophet an unusual experience which I believe signifies the reality of the diverse degrees of glory we can walk in.

In this account, the Lord led the prophet to the entrance of the temple where Ezekiel saw water coming out from under the threshold of the temple. As he stepped into the water in obedience to divine instructions, the water was ankle deep. Adhering to instructions, he went further and the water increased to knee level. Then it came up to his waist, and afterward it became an overwhelming river to swim in.

The flow of the river of God in the life of a believer is similar to this experience of the prophet. The further we go, the deeper the glory we encounter.

Some years ago when I was just a young believer, I noticed that some Christians seem to make the Bible story come alive by the extraordinary manifestations of God in and through their lives. The presence of God seems to be flowing out of them to affect lives, and as I pondered this it stirred in me a strong quest for more of God.

Driven by this hunger I stumbled on two books by John Osteen which made a lot of difference in my life, *The Super Supernatural* and *Divine Flow.*

As I consumed the contents of the two books I saw that it is not just enough to be desperate; my eyes were enlightened to understand the flow of the water from under the threshold of the temple as found in Ezekiel 47. As I approached the closing pages of the books, I decided to take some time out to wait on the Lord with fasting and prayer.

In order to get an appropriate atmosphere, I left school early. (During this period our neighborhood was usually very quiet.) When I got home, my passion became stronger and my expectation soared. I made up my mind to pray for at least one hour, trusting God to give me a similar experience.

I prayed with all my heart hoping, but at the expiration of one hour nothing spectacular had happened. A feeling of disappointment tried to overshadow me, but I made up my mind to rejoice in the fact that I was able to spend one hour in prayer besides the time spent studying the books and Ezekiel 47. As I was about to grip the door handle to leave that room, something strange happened. I heard these words, "Stand here and pray for fifteen minutes." It was not an audible voice yet it was so real, so I obeyed, just adoring and thanking God because by then I was done with my prayer points.

After a while, I began to feel a tingling sensation from the sole of my feet up to the ankle level. I wanted to ignore it, thinking it must have been a result of my standing for quite some time, but then something amazing happened. The sensation started moving up, and as I watched it got up to my knees and stopped. Now for sure I knew something unusual was happening to me, but just to confirm it I decided to watch out for what would happen next. And to my surprise it moved up to my waist and then stopped just as I had read from the book of Ezekiel. I continued praying, but I tell you the truth, my prayers were far from anything coherent because something amazing was happening to me. Suddenly it surged through me like a mighty wave and I knew this was it. Words are too inadequate to explain what I experienced that day, and after that encounter I was never the same.

It became my utmost joy to find time to be with the Lord. From that day onward as I fellowshipped with the Lord, I would feel the rushing of God's river through my body and there would be goose-bumps all over. The hair on my skin stood like hands lifted in worship, and as it passed they would fall flat again like a crowd bowing down in worship. It was an awesome sight to behold. My time of personal worship became more exciting and so precious to me. It became a thing of great joy just to stay there in God's presence. Until the Lord was through I was not through. It was the dawn of a new season in my life.

It is at such moments the song "Take Me Deeper" by Don Moen comes alive and I can truly sing with him from my heart:

Take me deeper
Deeper in love with you
Jesus hold me close to your embrace
Take me deeper
Deeper than I've ever been before
I just want to love you more and more
I long to be deeper Lord[10]

You can literally feel the presence of God upon your life if you are truly willing to love and glorify Him.

Everything You Touch Shall Live
In Ezekiel 47, when the water became a river too great for Ezekiel to swim in, he was lifted by the Lord to the bank of the

river. At this point the Lord said something very significant to him that we need to pay attention to. The Lord said,

> The river flows east through the desert into the Jordan Valley, where it enters the Dead Sea. The waters of this stream will heal the salty waters of the Dead Sea and make them fresh and pure. Everything that touches the water of this river will live. Fishermen will stand along the shores of the Dead Sea, fishing all the way from En-gedi to En-eglaim. The shores will be covered with nets drying in the sun. Fish of every kind will fill the Dead Sea just as they fill the Mediterranean![11]

This passage excites me. As we examine the above scripture, you will see that there is more to this river than its literal meaning. There is a spiritual angle to all of this.

First of all, don't forget that this river is said to be from the temple of the Lord, and in verse 8 we are told that this river flowed eastward. This flow was strong enough to push its way through the desert into the Jordan Valley. Now let's consider the spiritual significance.

First Corinthians 6:19 tells us the believer is the temple of the Holy Spirit. Beyond the Holy Spirit residing in us, it is His desire to fill us with His presence to overflowing till the world can encounter the glory of God through us. The Lord Jesus once spoke of rivers of living water flowing out of the belly of thirsty souls (John 7:38-39). From Revelation 22:1 we are made to understand that in heaven the personality of the Holy Spirit is also revealed as a river of the water of life, flowing out of the throne of God (the Father) and of the Lamb (Jesus). Therefore, the water God showed Ezekiel speaks of the manifestations of the Holy Spirit, and the temple is the believer hungry for God.

In Ezekiel, we are also told that the flow of this river went through the desert into the Jordan Valley. What does this mean? This is symbolic of the manifestations of the Spirit as He moves through us. Whenever it comes in contact with those who are depressed, confused, frustrated, weary, and hopeless (symbolic of the Jordan Valley) it will lift them out of their state of despondency. "Every valley shall be exalted...and the glory of the Lord shall be revealed, and all flesh shall see it together...."[12]

Whenever this river comes in contact with a person or a place that is spiritually dead (the desert), they will become flooded with the life of the Spirit.

When the river made its way to the Dead Sea where no life exists due to the high density of salt, the salty waters were healed and it became fresh and pure. The Dead Sea with its salty water signifies religious houses or churches that have been overtaken by traditions, rituals, philosophies, intellectualism, and the like. They have been very busy but unable to transform the lives of their devotees. They speak of it but are unable to show the beauty of the glory of the Lord. Their legalism and form only brought darkness and death. They are as dead as the Dead Sea because they are dead to the life of the Spirit. But as the river of God flows in, it is able to make it fresh and pure again, for where the Spirit of the Lord is the people become free (2 Corinthians 3:17).

Everything the river touches shall live. By this an entire congregation, community, city, and even a nation can be transformed. When this happens, then God's servants (the fishermen) will be able to stand along the shores of that which was once dead to fish as fishers of men, bringing souls into the kingdom of God.

Saturated with Glory

Your continual hunger, longing, and desperate desire for the presence of God is the key to usher you into the most intimate and glorious experience of life. As more of the Lord rubs off on you, His glory will begin to emerge from you. You will carry with you the fragrance of God's presence everywhere you go, and amazing things will begin to happen.

Any man who has spent time in a room saturated with smoke, incense, or perfume does not need to argue that he has been there because his body will reek of the content of that room. Those who help create an atmosphere of worship have often spent enough time in that atmosphere themselves. As they step out, the fragrance is strong enough to captivate people and sweep them off their feet, causing a feeling of awe, reverence, and deep hunger for more of God.

But as for those in the flesh, their reaction is different. The Amplified version of the Bible puts it this way:

> for we are the sweet fragrance of Christ [which exhales] unto God, [discernible alike] among those who are being saved and among those who are perishing: to the latter it is an aroma [wafted] from death to death [a fatal odor, the smell of doom]; to the former it is an aroma from life to life [a vital fragrance, living and fresh]. And who is qualified [fit and sufficient] for these things? [Who is able for such a ministry? We?][13]

While some are pleasantly drawn to it, hoping to have a drink from this fountain of life, others will move away becoming resentful, angry, jealous, antagonistic, and obnoxious, not wanting anything to do with it. They prefer to remain in their deadness and darkness because their deeds are evil (John 3:19). But as for those who are saturated with the glory of God, it is difficult for them to walk into a place without making a significant impact.

An Answer to Dangerous Religious Zeal

Some people are more concerned about dead traditions, laws, rituals, and religious creeds than they are about the heartbeat of God to seek out worshippers in spirit and truth. They jealously guard the shadow leaving the substance. They can be very devoted and ready to fight or kill anyone who attempts to touch or change the status quo about their religion. They are motivated by the same spirit that moved Saul to seek out, persecute, and slay Christians simply because their worship had become a threat to the traditions he loved so dearly. But on his way to Damascus to wreak greater havoc he met his Waterloo. He encountered Christ and understood by revelation the heavenly agenda, and he became the one mightily used by God to turn men from dead religious form and traditions to the light of the gospel. In his letter to Timothy, he classified people with mere religious zeal as "having a form of godliness but denying its power...."[14]

People with mere religious zeal can be dangerous, but this glory is too powerful for anyone to ignore. I have seen many religious hardliners who were determined to fight against the move of God swept off their feet and humbled by the Lord. When you encounter the glorious presence of the Lord, if you refuse to willingly bow in worship, you will be broken to pieces. It is when some are on the ground licking their wounds that they learn to worship in spirit and in truth. The good news is that when they get back on their feet, they are usually ready to worship with great reverence.

Saul, the religious fanatic who later became known as Paul, after his Damascus Road encounter became so anointed by God that mighty and special manifestations of the power and presence of the Lord accompanied his ministry (Acts 19:11-12).

He became so passionate for Jesus that he was ready to take any risk to help others encounter true worship. This is why he could say, "...whatever was to my profit I now consider loss for the sake of Christ....I want to know Christ and the power of his resurrection and the fellowship of sharing in his sufferings, becoming like him in his death."[15]

This Paul fell passionately in love with Jesus, and in return the Lord gave him divine insight and profound revelations to write more than half of the sacred books of the New Testament.

It is useless to argue and fight against religious hardliners. Just let them encounter the awesome presence of Jesus and they will be ready to go all the way for God.

It is not difficult for the Lord to do this Himself, but most of the time He just needs some of His saints on earth to be sensitive enough to identify with His passion for mankind and the world to see His glory.

It is in the place of worship, in deep and intimate communion with the Lord, that we learn to serve Him better.

It Equips the Body to Worship

When this river is flowing in the life of a local church, it helps to equip the members to become extraordinarily gifted for the work of the ministry with exceptional results (Ephesians 4:11-12). While others are struggling to do it by power and might, they will be cruising along by the grace of the Spirit.

The Scripture says, "If the iron be blunt, and he do not whet the edge, then must he put to more strength: but wisdom is profitable to direct."[16]

In every ministry of a church life, the Lord wants to deposit gifts in people who will become great assets to the body of Christ to help create an atmosphere of worship. The Lord is willing to help us if we are willing to ask Him and patiently follow Him.

In most churches, the music ministry is a thorn in the flesh. It is often plagued with lack of commitment, lack of capable hands, and, worst of all, the spirits of pride and immorality. The reason for this is not farfetched. Most church leaders are not patient enough to build the music ministry. They want to catch up with the Joneses and be known as the best in town. So being driven by a spirit of competition rather than worshipping in spirit and in truth, they quickly employ the best hands they can get, even if this means stealing the gifts of other churches by luring them away with attractive financial rewards and other benefits, not being careful to know how intimate such persons are with God. Now, because these guys came on board as lords or sacred cows, they become puffed up with pride and are insubordinate, undisciplined, insolent, and unserious.

They enjoy drawing attention to themselves with little or no concern about lifting others spiritually. The spirit behind their performance is entertainment and not worship. They pay little or no attention to the Word of God or prayer. This is why they are either passive or outside during the time of such important spiritual activities. And, true to their type, whenever these guys receive a better offer, they will be on the move again.

Unfortunately, many unsettled leaders refuse to learn. They would rather rush out again to steal from somewhere else than seek God's leading.

Jesus did not involve anyone who had not been with Him for a while in the work of His ministry. He called the Twelve from among those who had spent quality time with Him. We can even learn more from the reason why He called the Twelve. The first reason the Scripture gives is that "he ordained twelve that they should be with him,"[17] and then "that he might send them forth to preach"[18] was added.

Except we take time to see that those playing one role or the other in our worship experience are people who have been with the Lord, and as such channels by which the river of life flows, we are in trouble.

You can't give what you don't have. They may play or sing skillfully, but it will be empty. It may sound beautiful, but it will lack the power to impart life. It is "'Not by might nor by power, but by my Spirit,' says the LORD Almighty."[19]

If we will patiently wait on the Lord by yielding all to the Holy Spirit, He will work wonders beyond our imaginations and that river of life will flow to overwhelm us each time we worship.

All musicians, singers, and other worship leaders must be seen to be people who have developed a passionate and intimate relationship with the Lord before they are given the opportunity to lead.

If their heart does not overflow with such love for the Master, there will be problems. If the love of money or the praise of man is the passion behind any person, there will be problems.

God is not in need of talented or gifted people. He is looking for worshippers. If He finds one who truly worships in spirit and in truth, He is able to open their understanding and fill them with abilities they know nothing about. I have seen this happen to people as I committed myself to build up people to truly worship God in spirit and in truth.

If He did it for Bezaleel and Aholiab, as found in Exodus 31:1-6, He can do it for you. Just live to bring Him glory and you will be amazed what the King of Glory will do in and through you.

The Restoration of the Glory

Glory rested on the first man, Adam, before his fall in Eden. By this fall, Paul the apostle said the whole human race sinned and was stripped of the glory of God. We Christians were once among "all who have sinned and fallen short," alienated from the glory of God (Romans 3:23 and 5:12). But now, having received Christ Jesus, who is the second Adam, we have a better glory.

> For God who said, Let light shine out of darkness, has shone in our hearts so as [to beam forth] the light for the illumination of the knowledge of the majesty and glory of God [as it is manifest in the person and is revealed] in the face of Jesus Christ (the Messiah). However, we possess this precious treasure [the divine light of the Gospel] in [frail, human] vessel of earth, that the grandeur and exceeding greatness of the power may be shown to be from God and not from ourselves.[20]

We now carry about the glorious presence of God, to beam forth, illuminate, manifest, and reveal the very person of Jesus Christ to the world. Anyone who has given his or her life to Christ Jesus already has the potential to walk in and manifest the glory. This person has been empowered to walk in the awesome glory of God as a wonder to his or her generation (Colossians 1:27). Anything short of the manifestation of this glorious splendor is a waste of heaven's resources and frustration of divine purpose.

If you will open up to Him, the light of His glorious presence will shine in your heart and burn in you a fresh fire to worship until you are consumed with a passion to show forth the glory and majesty of our God and King. You are welcome to the glory of His presence.

CHAPTER THIRTEEN

HIS AWESOME PRESENCE AND GLORY

We often exclaim in awe whenever we suddenly encounter the incomprehensible and extraordinary. This feeling of trepidation or devotion stirred up from within our soul is a response beyond the intellect. In an atmosphere of worship, this would be the first clue of an audible response of this soul to God's call to worship. This is where the celestial and the terrestrial are integrated and mortals are ushered into the realm of the Immortal. As this soul is allowed to catch a glimpse of divinity, worship is born. It then receives the grace to engage in a spiritual dialogue as it gains access into the realm of the supernatural. It is in this realm that we see and hear things too awesome for the human intellect to translate into comprehensible language, but right here our spirit man becomes elated because it has gained entrance into that which is meant to be the natural abode of our eternal being.

It was in such moments of glory that men like Isaiah became so mesmerized to cry out, "Woe is me! For I am undone...for mine eyes have seen the King, the Lord of hosts."[1] His eyes saw the glory of the Almighty, and suddenly all his theology and reasoning became inadequate.

The prophet Ezekiel said, "...when I saw it I fell upon my face..."[2] and when he was told to stand on his feet he could not. His human nature had been overwhelmed by the glorious presence, and this became his doorway into a prophetic ministry.

When this door was opened to Daniel, he was able to access things hidden to the wisdom of men and so received insight about mysteries and the end of time (Daniel 8:15-18).

When John encountered this presence on the Island of Patmos, he said, "When I saw him, I fell at his feet as though dead..."[3] and it was this encounter that gave birth to the book of Revelation.

This is still happening all over the world as our God manifests Himself in the affairs of mortals. This is where we are able to access the revelation that grants us insight and understanding to the divine mysteries of ages and we become a wonder. That the angelic beings now have to depend on mortals (born into the dispensation of grace) to understand the mysteries of the ages makes it really amazing (Ephesians 3:1-5). True worship can never be the drudgery people are made to go through—it is awe-inspiring and eternal.

It's a Divine Encounter

For the soul that has come to know God's awesome presence and glory, worship is more than a special day of the week or a carefully planned liturgy. It is no longer just one of those events or a special religious gathering. It is a delightful anticipation of the divine romance and ecstasy that awaits one in a divine fellowship. To this soul, no distance or challenge is a strong enough hindrance to keep him away from the true passion of his soul. Without doubt, a moment with the Creator of the heavens and the earth, the planetary bodies, and the carefully arranged galaxies must be an unfathomable encounter. When David the psalmist found himself in this position, he was moved to exclaim:

> O Lord our God,
> How majestic is your name in all the earth
> You have set your glory above the heavens

> When I consider your heavens, the work
> of your fingers, the moon and stars,
> which you have set in place
> What is man that you are mindful of him
> the son of man that you care for him?[5]

The hymn writer puts it this way:

> O Lord my God, when I in awesome wonder
> Consider all the works thy hands have made
> I see the stars, I hear the rolling thunder,
> Thy power throughout
> the universe displayed.
>
> Then sings my soul my saviour God to Thee;
> How great Thou art, how great Thou art
> Then sings my soul my saviour God to Thee.
> How great Thou art,
> How great Thou art![6]

The glorious majesty, power, and complexity displayed by the hand of the Creator all over creation are enough to cause one to bow in reverence of the Most High. Just to know that you have been ushered into the very presence of the King of the universe is too much for our finite mind to comprehend and too overwhelming for our frail being to stand. This is where most people logout (pass out).

When the children of Israel encountered it on Mount Sinai, the Scripture says, "...there was thunder and lightning, with a thick cloud over the mountain, and a very loud trumpet blast. Everyone in the camp trembled."[7]

And before they could recover from this, "Mount Sinai was covered with smoke, because the Lord descended on it in fire. The smoke billowed up from it like smoke from a furnace, the whole mountain trembled violently and the sound of the trumpet grew louder and louder."[8]

They could not stand it. From a safe distance they "...said to Moses, 'speak to us yourself and we will listen. But do not have God speak to us or we will die.'"[9]

The presence was too awesome for their natural being to stand so they chose to alienate themselves from the manifest presence and glory of God rather than die of fear. It is true that no flesh can stand in the presence of God, but a soul that has come into an intimate relationship with God can walk into the cloud of glory like Moses did and feel love and reverence instead of horror (Exodus 19:20). If we go in our spirit and not our flesh, it will be far from a frightful experience. It will be a glorious encounter.

We are alienated from the presence and glory of God when we have no intimate relationship with God. Our spiritual disorder can become a terrible hindrance in our attempt to access the presence of God.

All those who have been redeemed and justified by the atonement of Jesus have been given access to the awesome presence of the Father by the Holy Spirit. That not withstanding, when this same soul encounters a greater degree of glory in the presence of the Lord, it cannot but fall down and worship in awe like John did in Revelation 1:17.

Like a Mighty Surge of Electricity

I have personally come to the conclusion that when most people sing "Touch me one more time, O Lord" they have no idea what they are asking for. In case you are wondering what I mean, let me explain to you from my own experience. It all happened over fifteen years ago when I was alone in my mother's provision store where I was to spend the night. This particular store had just one window that was never opened (due to the items on display), a big door, and a few fancy blocks that were meant to give additional ventilation but had been blocked to keep away mice. You can imagine how difficult it was to get a comfortable sleep in such a place, but on this night I did not care because I was caught up in a sweet communion with God.

By the time I thought I was through, I wanted to rest my head on the pillow to get some sleep because it was already past midnight, but the joy of this sweet fellowship moved me to plant my knees on the bed, and I began to tell the Lord how much I loved and needed Him. I believe I must have said, "Lord, please do something special for me," and suddenly I felt a gentle but well-focused wind on my forehead. I immediately knew this was something out of the ordinary because there was no way that could be happening with the door and window shut and the fancy blocks blocked. Before I could figure it out, a presence so overwhelming like a mighty surge of electricity overpowered me and I was knocked unconscious.

It happened so fast there was no time for me to even scream or reason it out. I thought I was dying, but when I later gained consciousness I could hear the voices of neighbors outside. I looked at the clock and was amazed to find out that it was already 6 a.m. As I struggled to a sitting position I asked in fear, "Lord, what was that?" Then it dawned on me that I had spent over six hours awestruck, yet it felt like two minutes ago. It was so powerful and yet so terrifying that I was afraid to say, "Lord, touch me one more time."

If you have ever truly encountered the awesome and glorious presence of the Lord, you will agree that there is nothing like it. Nothing in this whole world comes close to it. It is for the lack of appropriate words that we say "it is like a mighty surge of electricity." His presence brings such glorious transformation to a soul that it cannot be ignored. After such an encounter you will be able to understand why some people are so crazy and passionate after the presence of God. Sometimes all one needs to become desperate for God is just a touch from above. This is when songs like "Breathe" by Michael W. Smith become meaningful and so appropriate to help this passionate worshipper express his/her longing for more of the awesome presence of God.

If you have the time to meditate on the text of this song, coupled with the music, you will agree that this must have come from a heart that had been touched from above. Part of the song says,

> This is the air I breathe
> Your holy presence living in me
>
> This is my daily bread
> Your very word spoken to me
>
> And I ___ I'm desperate for you
> And I ___ I'm lost without you[4]

A Regular Phenomenon of Awe

To worship in spirit and in truth is to live in a realm of awe, and this is meant to be a regular phenomenon, the frequency of occurrence notwithstanding. This is the reason the angels round about the throne of God can't stop crying day and night:

> Holy, Holy, Holy, Lord God Almighty, which was and is, and is to come. And when those beasts give glory and honor and thanks to him that sat on the throne, who liveth for ever and ever, the four and twenty elders fall down before him that sat on the throne and worship him that liveth for ever and ever and cast their crowns before the throne, saying Thou art worthy O Lord, to receive glory and honor and power for thou hast created all things and for thy pleasure they are and were created.[10]

If you can always see Him, you can always worship. This is not the worship that is motivated by any form or creed. It is provoked deep from within our spirit to honor and reverence Him who alone is worthy of worship.

The awesome manifestation of God's presence transcends culture, nationality, and the reasoning of mortals. In Nigeria, one of the songs that easily lifts us to the conscious reality of

His awesome presence is "Awesome God, Mighty God." The text of this song, though simple and short, when rendered repeatedly creates an atmosphere with such electrifying effect. Here's the lyric:

Awesome God, mighty God (2x)
We give you praise, mighty God.
You are highly lifted up, awesome God (2x)[11]

Most of the time people are unable to see God's awesomeness because they have been blinded by religious cloaks, traditions, and carnality. The power of darkness is working hard to keep men from the conscious reality of our God, but this is a futile venture, for the earth shall become full of the knowledge of God and His glory as the waters cover the sea (Habakkuk 2:14).

There is more to the manifest presence of God than you have known. A greater glory awaits any soul truly passionate for God.

This is where all troubles, cares, and pains are reduced to shadows in the light of His glorious presence. In this realm, worship with fresh passion is a pleasant response to God's call to worship. Right here all who seek for God with their whole heart will find Him. "The Spirit and the bride say, 'come!' and let him who hears say, 'come!' Whoever is thirsty, let him take the free gift of the water of life."[12]

To walk with the King of Glory is to dwell in a regular phenomenon of awe, but the choice is yours.

CHAPTER FOURTEEN

KEEPING IT FRESH

༄ྀ

> The steadfast love of the Lord never ceases.
> His mercies never come to an end. They are
> new every morning, new every morning.
> Great is thy faithfulness O Lord. Great is thy
> faithfulness.[1]

The words you just read are the text of a well-known worship song among Christians (Lamentations 3:22-23). Prior to these two verses, the prophet speaking as a voice for the nation of Israel lamented their misery, afflictions, helplessness, limitations, and other forms of suffering, but just then he saw a ray of hope at the remembrance that the unfailing love of the Lord never ceases and that His mercies are new every morning.

Each time I sing this song, I rejoice in the fact that "they are new every morning." Therefore, it does not matter how bad yesterday was, we can always count on God for fresh love and mercies every morning. Hallelujah! Nobody wants to have anything to do with something that is stagnant. We all want something fresh or new. Anything stagnant can be very dangerous to the environment and the health of man. Anything stagnant is often unpleasant in appearance and offensive in smell. It is more often than not very dirty.

People have a natural tendency to go for that which is fresh, new, or most recent as opposed to that which is stale or outdated.

The aroma of fresh bread cannot be compared to that of yesterday. Just as fresh fruits and vegetables are preferred to those that are old and weak, fresh flowing water is preferred over a stagnant pond. In like manner, fresh and passionate worship is preferred over dead tradition and religion.

The Wisdom of the Uncivilized

In Africa, most villages depend on streams, rivers, and waterfalls for drinking water, and the people are careful enough to be sure the source of this water is always flowing and free from any contamination. To keep the water source fresh, it is forbidden to do laundry or toilet there. They may not have fertilizers and the various scientific means to improve their farm produce, yet they are wise enough to have days and seasons set aside to rest the land and their bodies. The outside world may see this people as uncivilized, but they have the simple wisdom that guarantees bumper harvests. They are effectively managing the resources that nourish their souls. Not many in the civilized world are that wise, hence a great number fall sick and die from the side effects of farm chemicals and industrial waste.

In the same way, so many sophisticated Christians are drinking from contaminated pools. Too many religious gatherings feed the souls of their devotees with toxic materials instead of nourishing their souls. When we turn our eyes from the Lord, who is the fountain of life, and focus them on our methods, traditions, and skills, we make the soul sick.

As we unwittingly repeat our order of worship over and over again, we breed a people passionate after religious forms but not after God.

When the content of our worship is not initiated by the Holy Spirit but by the influence and desires of certain individuals, it will lack the power to stir people to worship fervently. Mere religious zeal lacks the power to transform any life, but the man with a fresh word from the altar of God will be able to make people worship till they are overwhelmed with a divine glow.

Sometimes it is hard to understand how an unlearned man is able to produce extraordinary results where those who are trained, certified, and polished struggle. Well, the truth is that the one considered unlearned, like those uncivilized villagers, saw the need to depend totally on the true source of divine revelations, but the learned depend and pride themselves on their abilities and the prestige of their great institution.

Similarly, many religious people would rather worship their tradition than let God have His way. They seem to be afraid that the leading of the Spirit will mess up their carefully planned order of service. It is the "As it was in the beginning, is now and ever shall be" mentality. People came to the stream hoping to find fresh water to refresh their souls only to find a dry riverbed, and so they return spiritually empty and famished.

When the worship leaders themselves are a dry riverbed, the plants growing on its bank (people who come to worship) will soon wither away. When a leader fails to draw from the fountain of life, he will have no option but to feed his parishioners with dead religious form (stagnant water). Those who rigidly follow that which was handed to them from one generation to another would at best build an irrelevant institution. This is where I have a problem with the song that says, "Give me that old time religion, it's good enough for me." The problem here is that what many consider "the old time religion" is only a form devoid of the life and power that makes the difference. There is a greater glory for us in this generation. You will have to reason like a fool, like the uncivilized, to be able to access it.

The Empty Pride of the Samaritan

The Samaritan woman in John 4 believed nothing else compared to the water from Jacob's well. She belonged to the class of those who believe their tradition is superior to that of others because it can be traced back to some outstanding heroes and patriarchs. They refuse to believe there can be something better, and by so doing they limit God.

As Jesus spoke with this woman, she began to see the emptiness and shallowness of her tradition. She suddenly realized that the tradition she had been drinking from for many years had not been able to quench the true thirst of her soul. For the first time she learnt of the water that can both quench her thirst and become in her a well of water springing up into everlasting life. Suddenly the scales of tradition fell off her eyes and she let out the true yearning of her soul, "Sir, give me this water so that I won't get thirsty and have to keep coming here to draw water."[2]

And she got it. If we will lead men to the true source of life that is always fresh and pure, they will have no need for that which has become stale.

God, speaking through His servant Jeremiah, revealed to us His displeasure with dead traditions when He said,

> "Be appalled at this, O heavens, and shudder with great horror," declares the Lord. "My people have committed two sins: They have forsaken me, the spring of living water, and have dug their own cisterns, broken cisterns that cannot hold water."[3]

Our dead traditions and lifeless religious forms are the broken cisterns that cannot satisfy the longing of the soul because they lack the manifest presence of God. People who have to put up with this often lack the joy and satisfaction of a life well-nourished in God. When the people discover how dry the brook has become they will walk away in search of the true fountain of life.

A Stifled Atmosphere of Worship

When most people walk through the doors from the contaminated atmosphere of the world, they hope to breathe some fresh air of life in our worship. For many, this is the last gas station they had in mind or else their hope will fade into oblivion. Many who make it to this place of worship do so in the hope of finding rest for their weary souls, but it is unfortunate that some worship experiences only help to choke life out of weak and wounded souls.

The fact that people gather for what we call "worship service" week in and week out does not mean they have been able to find true worship. The use of songs, prayers, and exhortation in a gathering is not a guarantee that worship took place. We must realize that worship is not items or activities lined up in a religious gathering. Worship transcends mere religious rites and liturgical forms. If we observe closely we will discover that people have been sneaking away unnoticed. Propelled by an innate desire for more of the life that comes from God, they cannot help but wander from pillar to post.

The strength and pressure by which water flows from a hose depends on its firm connection to the source. Any worship experience characterized by a true and sincere passion gives us a clue of the degree of intimacy between the worship leaders and the Lord. In such a place, it is not uncommon to find beautiful expressions of love, peace, and ecstasy that are real.

Protecting the Destiny of the Next Generation

Through the ages, churches have been closed down or even converted into mosques, Hindu temples, department stores, and city monuments due to the lack of focus of church leaders. Just one careless preparation for worship can be so dangerous to the destiny of a generation.

In the fifth and sixth centuries, while the church leaders were busy fighting over position, power, sectional doctrine, and other trivial issues, a more ambitious Islamic group was taking over major parts of North Africa, Jerusalem, Eastern Europe, the Middle East, and Asia. Subsequently, that generation and many others became subject to the brutal slavery of lifeless traditions and religion. Most of these places have been under the strong grip of Islam and other religions for many years now.

Today there are churches in Europe and some parts of the Western world struggling to fill their magnificent edifices and cathedrals. In them you will find only a few traditional hardliners who are nothing but the smoldering wick of an old lamp as it ebbs away. Unless there is a drastic change such places will soon become history.

In some of these places, the worship has become stale and irrelevant to the young and upcoming generation thanks to too much emphasis on traditions and denominational segregation.

Most young guys today are passionate about football but very passive about church activities. Just in case you are wondering why, you need to pay a visit to a live football match. In the football arena, you can tell that the fans have come in with a lot of expectation, and as they express their passion for their team, the arena becomes charged. The liberty with which people express themselves in arenas like this knows no bounds. Sometimes they can become so wild just to show their passion for the game they love. They can predict how explosive a particular game will be by the knowledge of the teams and players on parade, especially when they have information about the deliberate efforts and strategies employed during training. When the game finally commences, every fan looks forward to see their team make good its promise, and when they score a point, it is spontaneously celebrated by a jubilant and passionate response from the fans.

A serious fan cannot afford to see this team beaten because his/her ego and pride is greatly attached to the performance of the team. It is not just a game to them; the victory of their team has become their personal victory, hence they cannot help but cheer on with passion. If they have to travel long distances, spend heavily, and stay awake into odd hours of the night just to support the team, they are ready to go all the way.

On the contrary, most churches have not been able to get these same people who are members of their local assembly to become this passionate about worship. They seem not to understand why they have to forsake other commitments for a worship service. Therefore, whenever a football game clashes with a church worship, the church attendance will become scanty.

We are gradually seeing the rise of a generation that is more a lover of pleasure (sport) than lovers of God. There are now places where the sporting arena and other venues of entertainment are jam-packed, leaving many church pews empty.

Until our worship becomes an encounter which satisfies the true yearning and passion of the souls of men, we will continually struggle to keep them in church.

The answer is not in the theories of a thousand and one seminars and conferences on "How to take your church to the next level." Until you get to the next level yourself you cannot show others the way. Get on your knees before God and you will encounter His awesome presence; extraordinary results will follow.

If we are able to keep a fresh and passionate communion with God, we will soon possess enough fire that the spiritually cold will come to get baptized with fresh fire from above.

Our corporate fellowship will then produce one mighty flame that can be seen from afar, stirring the hearts of many to come seeking the visitation that is from above. As this flame spreads we will see old department stores, warehouses, and city halls converted to places of worship as hungry souls cry out to God. There is nothing like the breath of God to a soul overwhelmed by the troubles of life. With so much stress, sorrow, terror, disappointment, uncertainty, treachery, dishonesty, corruption, and evil scheming to steal the joy of living, nothing but the fresh breath from the presence of God can soothe us.

A religious meeting saturated with intellectualism but devoid of reverential awe is not worship. Emphasis on intellectualism is the celebration of the glory of man, but emphasis on a divine encounter with our heavenly Father is to contemplate and commune with the divine mystery of the Godhead and the essence of our being.

That which originates in the head of man can only gain access to the intellect and emotions of man. But that which is from the Spirit can navigate its way into the spirit of man, overwhelming that soul with a passion to worship in spirit and in truth. This is the realm and arena of worship.

CHAPTER FIFTEEN

FINDING THE PASSION TO WORSHIP AGAINST ALL ODDS

Sometimes to worship with passion can be quite a challenge. There are nights we go to bed pondering how to navigate our way out of a nagging problem or situation, hoping for a miracle, only to wake up the next morning to see the problem staring us in the face.

There are times when all our prayers, positive confessions, and attitudes are rebuffed by the realities of the present darkness. Sometimes the problems of life compel people to ask, "Why do bad things happen to good people?"

To promise people a life without trouble on earth is to give them a false hope. That would be living life on Fantasy Island, but in the real world trouble is a part of life.

If life is not a bed of roses and troubles are inevitable, how then can one find the passion to always worship? It is expected of us to rejoice for evermore (1 Thessalonians 5:17), but what does this really mean? Does it mean a church is expected to worship with great excitement after their faithful friend and pastor loses his lovely and supportive wife?

After a church gets the news that some of their members who went on a mission trip have died in a tragic accident, will it be normal to find them shouting and dancing with great joy during their next worship experience?

Just how do you expect a young woman to express herself in worship after she hears that the guy she is madly in love with is having a serious affair with another woman?

What if a Christian who has been faithful in giving and service to the Lord suddenly receives news of the loss of all his investment? Is the presence of pain the absence of true worship?

When the emotions of people have been deeply wounded, it is normal for such souls to struggle to get back to that realm of bliss and great comfort they once knew in worship. If worship is truly with all our heart, all our soul, and all our strength, then without doubt an emotionally wounded soul will struggle to worship.

For this soul, the present circumstances and situations seem to have succeeded in stifling his/her passion to worship. Bewildered by such conditions, many have been forced to hide behind closed doors as gloom and sadness set in. After the death of Jesus, His disciples dealt with a similar circumstance. They had just witnessed their Lord and Master crucified without any opposition from heaven or earth. The emotional trauma they went through should have made them have trouble getting any sleep that night. The horror of their shattered dreams and lives was a terrible nightmare. Their hopes and the promise for a better life and future had been washed down the drain. It never crossed their minds that everything would come to such an abrupt end as it did. Everything was well on course before the religious leaders came to burst their bubble, and now it was not going to be easy to start all over again.

The fact that their deliverer and leader now lay stone dead in Joseph of Arimathea's tomb was enough psychological trouble. They could not reconcile all His supernatural manifestations, like the healings of the sick and the raising of the dead, with His death. Without doubt, these guys had taken more than their finite minds could handle, and in this state a worship service was way out of the question. Even on the very day of Jesus' resurrection, they were too disillusioned to worship. Their passion to worship was only ignited by the appearance of the Lord in their midst while the doors were shut (John 20:19-20).

Enthusiasm in worship is often a result of a sense of gratitude and a strong anticipation of better things to come. Therefore, to come to worship with a wounded soul and nothing tangible to look forward to is enough to deflate the enthusiasm of any soul.

In their state of despondency, it must have been difficult for the disciples to even weep. The loudest cry would be close to a whisper and the main song a dirge rendered under their breath. Not even the one overwhelmed with grief was permitted to do so out loud. Others would have been quick to say "Shh! Please keep it down" should he or she become too emotional. This was not a time of exhilaration. It was a time of deep pain and regrets.

In the 1980s, the popular song "By the Rivers of Babylon" by Bonny M. was a danceable song, but, taken from the scriptural account that chronicles the lamentation of the children of Israel in captivity, it was a song of sorrow.

As captive Israel sat by the river of Babylon, their captors required them to sing their joyful songs of worship and celebration just to entertain them, but in deep agony they replied, "How can we sing the Lord's song in a strange land?"[1]

The question "How can we sing...?" reveals to us the depth and degree of their emotional trauma. It was a big misfit for captives to sing joyful songs in a state of misery. One must be out of the natural realm to be able to sing songs of joy among such merciless and brutal Babylonians.

To find the passion to worship joyfully in despicable situations has always been a tough challenge. The disciples of Jesus were overwhelmed with fear, and consequently they became scattered like sheep without a shepherd.

And when they later met behind closed door, it was in fear, and no act of worship was recorded then. Even after they were well aware of Christ's resurrection, it was not easy for them to get back their enthusiasm to worship. There was this uncertainty about the future of the mission. An uneasy calm took over the camp, and when Peter finally spoke, he said, "I am going to fish." And the others said, "We will go with you"[2] This is a true picture of the depth of their confusion and lack of passion to continue what they were once ready to die for.

Proverbs says, "Hope deferred makes the heart sick..."[3] and when the heart is sick our worship becomes sick. People would rather while away the time in some form of pleasure or unfruitful venture than think of worship. This is when many pastors want to go fishing like Peter.

In the same way, today many worship leaders are substituting worship with recreation. Recreation cannot revive the spirit of a man; it will only bring temporal pleasure to the flesh, and it can never be enough.

The Ingredient of Courage

When things bring us gloom and sadness, leaders must remember the words of Jesus to Peter: "Feed my lambs."[4]

When people are low in spirit, it is difficult for them to listen to any sermon. The present reality seems to make a mockery of their hopes, and they experience what Henry Blackaby would call "crisis of belief." This is when we fail to realize that the worship offered in moments of darkness is actually the priceless evidence we need to validate and justify the extraordinary favors and blessing the Almighty designated to us. This worship speaks of the sacrifice of praise.

The Israelites by the river of Babylon could not see this, nor could the disciples of Jesus see it. Amazingly, in the peak of this misery, some of the women found courage to go to the tomb, hoping to at least anoint His body, and their boldness made a lot of difference. On the way, their major concern was "who will roll the stone away from the entrance of the tomb?"[5] That was the only obstacle they saw. The soldiers and the seal of Pilate was not an issue to them, but later this courage was rewarded with exhilarating worship.

In the courage of these women we discover a clue on how we can find the passion to worship against all odds. Their actions have taught us the following lessons:

1. We must find some courage to seek the Lord no matter the prevailing circumstance—even if it seems useless as in the case of the women who went seeking for one who had been certified dead. They had the hope to at least anoint His body. Job was able to say in his time of grief, "Though He slays me, yet will I hope in Him."[6] Even if it does not seem to make any sense, we must find some courage to worship.

2. Don't allow the fear and discouragements of others and prevailing circumstances to stop you. When there is no encouragement from those you thought should know better, go ahead. The women decided to go ahead when the men were too discouraged and terrified to step out. When you are incarcerated like the Israelites by the river of Babylon, don't hang your harp. Sing down the glory of God, and like Paul and Silas your praise will break the shackles off your feet (Acts 16:25-26).

3. If we will step out with courage, we will get to the tomb and find the stone (the obstacle) rolled away. We will then see that which was dead, alive with a greater glory. The psalmist said, "Weeping may last for a night, but a shout of joy comes in the morning."[7]

It may be your night season right now, but if you will find some courage to worship, after a while you will be overwhelmed with a great joy.

Cook Up Your Own Encouragement

The prophet Habakkuk in a period of much uncertainty had reason to say,

> Though the fig tree does not bud and there are no grapes on the vines, though the olive crop fails and the fields produce no food, though there are no sheep in the pen and no cattle in the stalls, yet I will rejoice in the Lord, I will be joyful in God my savior. The sovereign Lord is my strength; He makes my feet like the feet of the deer, He enables me to go on to the heights.[8]

This scripture was assigned to the director of music, so this must have been a song for worship. Don Moen did write a wonderful song based on this passage titled "I Will Sing." (More detail about this song can be found in the album *I Will Sing*.)

I believe that to be joyful is by choice and to sing is also by choice. If you make up your mind, no matter what, you will not only sing, you will worship with a fresh passion. If you have the confidence that God is faithful no matter what, you will worship.

"In 1904, Mrs. Civilla Martin, visited a friend who was bed ridden and asked her if she ever got discouraged because of her physical condition. Her friend responded quietly: 'Mrs Martin, how can I be discouraged when my heavenly father watches over each little sparrow and I know He loves and cares for me.'"[9] And within a short time, the inspiration to write the classic hymn "His Eye Is on the Sparrow" was given. This song has helped so many to worship against all odds.

No matter the odds against you, if you are able to come to the realization that His eyes are on you, you will find courage to worship.

I believe Darlene Zschech wrote the song "I Will Run to You" with the understanding that the Father cares so much for us and that He is always willing and ready to comfort us if we will turn to Him in our times of need. (You can find more detail about this song in Alvin Slaughter's album *Rain Down*.)

In the album *We Offer Praises*, Ron Kenoly sings a song by David Baroni titled "He's Been Good." Just listening to it reassures one that the Lord is always with us through the storms of life. A part of the song says,

> I have known the Father's care for me,
> He's been good, He's been good.
> Through it all He's always there for me,
> God's been good to me.[10]

(Go to the album *We Offer Praises* for more details about this song.)

The enemy knows that the joy of the Lord is your strength (Nehemiah 8:10 KJV), and this is the reason why he often attacks those things that bring you joy. When you see this happen, make sure you don't lose your joy; stay in the presence of God.

Ron Kenoly in his song "I Still Have Joy" testified to the fact that despite the enemy's plot to destroy our lives, we can triumph (see the album *We Offer Praises* for more details about this song). Your joy is in the presence of the Lord. Just stay there and you will be fine.

Worship, and God Will Fight Your Battle

The Word of the Lord says, "Hope deferred makes the heart sick."[11] Once the expectations of a man are shattered, he is suddenly gripped with fear and uncertainty. Especially when you have been praying all along, hoping things will work out fine. Your confidence melts away and you are confused. This is the point when we need to reassure ourselves that God is faithful. He has said, "Never will I leave you, never will I forsake you."[12]

Some years ago a brother went out with another Christian on what we call "two-by-two witnessing." In the process of this evangelical outing, they were confronted by a witchdoctor who cast a spell on this brother by touching him with his staff. The two Christians had not gone beyond a block when this brother experienced a strange feeling and suddenly had difficulty walking. In a matter of days, it grew worse as he began to have symptoms of paralysis. The brother became dejected. Fear and uncertainty were gaining ground as all efforts to proffer a solution by drugs yielded no positive result. We heard of it and arranged for him to be brought to the church. It was obvious this was a satanic attack and we should confront it by binding the powers of darkness, taking authority in Jesus' name. But then the Lord told us to simply worship Him by proclaiming His Lordship.

As we held our hands together, we worshipped the Lord with the brother in the middle of the circle. Amazingly, as we did this, within five minutes the brother who came in limping and shivering began to sweat heavily till his T-shirt was soaked. Suddenly he sprang up and dashed into the street shouting and praising God. "I am healed, I am healed, I am healed! Thank You, Jesus!" To Jesus be all the glory.

While we passionately gave praise to God the spell was broken, and this was because the Lord showed up. When we truly worship in spirit, there is no limit to what God can do.

In 2 Chronicles 20, when King Jehoshaphat heard that three nations were coming together against him in battle, he was overshadowed with fear. He knew there was no way he could defeat them in battle, but in his bewilderment he saw the need to seek God's face. He cried out to God saying,

> ...O LORD, God of our fathers, are you not the God
> Who is in heaven? You rule over all the kingdoms
> of the nations. Power and might are in your hand,
> and no one can withstand you....[13]

When he acknowledged that no one can withstand God, in Judah's time of trouble God took over his battle. By a prophetic word they went against their enemies singing praises unto God, and as they worshipped on the battleground their enemies began to fight against themselves until every one of them died.

When Jehoshaphat and the people of Judah got there, their only job was to carry the great wealth they met in the midst of their dead enemies, and it took them three days to do the job.

If we will learn to worship against all odds, we will see the glorious wonders of our God. What you think came to finish you is actually an opportunity for you to see God bless you like never before. So don't just stand there complaining, get your praise on and see the glory of God revealed for your good.

Apply the Attitude of Gratitude

The hymn writer Thomas O. Chisholm, in appreciation to God, wrote the all-time classic hymn "Great Is Thy Faithfulness." This wonderful song has stirred the hearts of so many to overcome their fears and uncertainties, giving them confidence for the future. By meditating on the lyrics of this song you will be moved to testify with the writer that God is faithful (see *The Baptist Hymnal 1991*, No. 54, for more details about the song).

Just to wake up each day to see that the sun is still there and the various blessings of creation are still available for us is enough to stir up a sense of gratitude. Our God is so faithful, and that is why Bob Fitts in his own way testified to this in the song "You Are So Faithful" (see *Bob Fitts and The Maranatha! Singers*). Sometimes we are so encumbered with the petty issues of life that we forget to be grateful for all the blessings that are ours from above.

A young man was once brought to my office with a health problem. He was having problems digesting everything he took in. As a result of this he became lean and weak because he had been running stool for over five months. As he told me his frustration with doctors and the fact that he had spent above his little earning, the Lord told me to tell him to spend seven days in thanksgiving and he would be fine. He looked at me in amazement because he thought it was a problem that had to do with satanic attack, and he was expecting us to bind demons. But when he went and did as instructed, on the third day I got a call testifying that he had been healed. It was by the attitude of gratitude that he got his healing. No hand was laid on him and no oil was poured on him. God did it when he showed gratitude.

Prophesy to Your Future

The song "God Will Make a Way" by Don Moen remains one of the most outstanding songs ever written to encourage the low in spirit, the wounded, and the brokenhearted. He said the inspiration to write this song came as he thought of the best way to encourage a close family member who just lost a loved one. I believe it was a prophetic word he received that became a comfort to all those hurting. Isaiah 43:18-19 will tell you more.

Sometimes all we need to move from depression to exhilaration is the courage to prophesy God's Word to our circumstances until we see them transformed into the prophetic declaration we have received from God.

Morris Chapman and the Maranatha! Singers sang a song titled "He Is Able." I have personally found some lifting again and again just prophesying this song to circumstances. Our God is able to do more than we can ever ask or think (Ephesians 3:20).

The psalmist prophesied to himself saying, "Bless the Lord, O my soul: And all that is within me bless his holy name."[14] He also said, "Why are you downcast, O my soul? Put your hope in God, for I will yet praise him, my saviour and my God."[15]

When he looked beyond the prevailing circumstance he was able to see the promise and faithfulness of God, so he prophetically said, "Praise awaits you, O God, in Zion."[16]

Shirley Caesar sang a song written by Dawn Thomas titled "He'll Do It Again," and just going through the words of this song will reassure you that "He'll do it again" (you can find details about this song in the album *I Remember Mama*).

Yes, you may not know when or how, but God will do it again. We must learn to prophesy to our circumstances. A popular prophetic song in Nigeria says,

I can see Him working in my favor
I can see Him fighting my battle,
I can see Him bringing in my miracles
He will do what He says He will do.[17]

Master Your Circumstances

The great composer Beethoven, just when he was developing great skills for the composition of music, began to lose his hearing. This was a nightmare too horrifying for any composer. To a musician, the ability to hear and appreciate the beauty of musical notes is one of his greatest assets. Without the hearing, composing music will become some form of drudgery; yet when his hearing ability was gone, he was able to master the art of composition and in the process earned for himself a place in the hall of fame among the great composers of all times. Here was a man who had every reason to become passive and indignant, yet he found reason to bring others pleasure. Though he was denied access to the inspiration available by the sounds of his surroundings, he made a difference in his world.

If only we will try to see the opportunities that exist in our misfortune, we will be able to find the courage to rise from the dust and ash of defeat to master our circumstances and situations as we soar on the wings of the Spirit.

You can make it if you try.

Worship Is Always by Faith

Fanny J. Crosby was said to have lived for over ninety years, but of this period she was only able to see for just the first six years of her life because she became blind through improper medical treatment. Yet through the eyes of faith she had the ability to see what others were blind to. It is said that one "Mrs. Knapp played a tune in Fanny's hearing once or twice and then asked her, 'What does that melody say to you?' and Fanny Crosby replied with the precise words, 'Blessed assurance, Jesus is mine! Oh what a foretaste of glory divine! Heir of salvation, purchase of God, born of His spirit, washed in his blood. This is my story, this is my song, praising my savior all the day long; this is my story, this is my song, praising my savior all the day long."[18]

This became stanza one of the hymn "Blessed Assurance" (HB p. 100). The amazing thing is the degree of vision she had in her physical blindness.

In the second stanza she wrote: "Perfect submission, perfect delight, visions of rapture now burst on my sight."[19] What a vision and what a sight this must have been to one others considered to be blind! In the third stanza she who was physically blind was able to write by faith, "Watching and waiting, looking above...."[20] She who had no physical sight had enough spiritual vision and confidence to call it "Blessed Assurance" (for the text go to *The Baptist Hymnal 1991*, No. 334). This should make some of us ask God for mercy.

So many who claim to have physical sight are just too blind to see the reason why they should worship. Jesus on several occasions healed people when He saw their faith, and He would sometimes add, "Your faith has made you whole."

All who can see through the eyes of faith should have no problem worshipping with a fresh passion in spirit and in truth, for worship is in the spirit.

A songwriter once wrote,

Let the living water flow over my soul
let the Holy Spirit come and take control
of every situation that has troubled my mind
all my cares and burdens unto him I roll[21]

No matter what the trouble is, if you will heed to the call of the Master, He will touch you, and out of your belly shall flow rivers of life. To worship is a matter of choice. You can find fresh passion to worship. You can access the realm of worship in spirit and in truth. When you do, your soul will then encounter true glory. His grace is enough for you. Shalom!

NOTES

Introduction: A Cry from Within

1. Psalm 23:2-3 NIV.
2. Corinthians 15:45, 48 NIV.

Chapter 1: Reminiscences of the First Encounter

1. C. Austin Miles, 1868-1946, "In the Garden" taken from *The Baptist Hymnal 1991*, No. 187.
2. Ibid.
3. A statement by Pastor E.A. Adeboye, the general overseer of The Redeemed Christian Church during the dedication of the Shekinah model parish in Warri, Delta state Nigeria.
4. See Acts 17:28 NIV.

Chapter 2: The Cold War over Worship

1. Karl Marx is well reputed for the statement "Religion is the opium of the people."
2. Kurt Kaiser is the writer of the song "Pass It On" which can be found in *The Baptist Hymnal 1991*.

Chapter 3: Where on Earth Is the Worshipping Church?

1. Germs from A.W. Tozer, extract from *The Writings of a 20th Century Prophet: The Missing Jewel of Worship*, p. 4.
2. A.W. Tozer, *Whatever Happens to Worship*, compiled and edited by Gerald B. Smith, p. 83.
3. Ibid. p. 85.
4. Internet source: http://liberry.thinkquest.org/1543/history/history-ren.htm
5. Internet source: http://wikipedia.org/wiki/Renaissance
6. A.W. Tozer, *Whatever Happens to Worship*, compiled and edited by Gerald B. Smith, p. 86.
7. See John 4:13-14 NIV.
8. See John 4:15 NIV.
9. See John 4:20 NIV.
10. Geoffrey Hanks, *70 Great Christians: The Story of the Christian Church*, p. 264.
11. Roberts Liardon, *God's Generals*, p.204.
12. Ibid. p. 204-205
13. Ibid. p. 205-220
14. See John 4:23-24 NLT.
15. See 1 Corinthians 1:3[b]
16. Ibid. v. 14.
17. See Matthew 23:15 NIV.
18. See 1 Chronicles 17:4-7 NASB .
19. 2 Chronicles 7:12 KJV.
20. See Jeremiah 7:13-15 NIV.
21. See Acts 17:24 NIV.
22. See John 21:15-17 NIV.
23. See Mark 13:2 NIV.
24. See 1 Kings 12:27, 33 NIV.
25. See John 7:37-38 NIV.
26. Don Harris, "Such Joy," taken from Hosanna! Music; *Come and Worship*, p.159.
27. Igho L. Yegbeburu wrote the song "Your Life" which was taken from *The Glory* album of The Glorious Fountain Ministries, 1997.

28. Rev. Kunle Oyeniyi's remark during the 2007 Worship Conference of The Glorious Fountain Ministries, Warri, Nigeria.
29. See Psalm 133:1 NIV.
30. See 1 Corinthians 12:4-6 NIV.
31. Cece Winans sang the song "Alabaster Box" taken from the album *Alabaster Box*.
32. See Colossians 3:15-17 NIV.

Chapter 4: Maximizing Our Precious Time of Worship

1. See 1 Samuel 16:7 NIV.
2. See 1 Corinthians 2:11-12 NIV.
3. 1 Corinthians 15:31 NIV.
4. Benny Hinn's comment about Kathryn Kuhlman taken from the video "Atmosphere for Miracles."
5. See Psalm 63:1-3 NIV.
6. Rick Warren's comment about Matt Redman's song "Heart of Worship" in his book *The Purpose Driven Life*, p.106.
7. A comment taken from the video "Great Souls" about Billy Graham's crusades in the UK.
8. See Matthew 11:28-30 NIV.
9. Lemmel H. Helen's song "Turn Your Eyes upon Jesus" taken from *The Baptist Hymnal 1991*, No. 320.
10. Taken from Rev. Dr. Paul Davidson's book *Come Let Us Worship*, p.2.
11. See Exodus 3:3 NIV.
12. See Isaiah 6:1-5 NIV.
13. Ibid.
14. The statement "I set myself on fire and people come to watch me burn" is credited to John Wesley.
15. See John 1:23 and Luke 3:16 NIV.
16. This is a story I heard from a friend during my seminary days.
17. See Job 39:19-25 NASB

18. See Psalm 45:1 NIV.
19. See 2 Corinthians 3:6 NIV.
20. Exodus 3:4 NIV.
21. The meaning of the word "dialogue" used in explaining the importance of divine dialogue in worship was taken from the *Oxford Advanced Learners' Dictionary*.
22. The *Scott, Foresman Intermediate Dictionary* is another source consulted in explaining the divine dialogue.
23. See Philippians 2:13 NIV.
24. See Luke 7:39 NIV.
25. See John 12:7 NIV.
26. Ecclesiastics 5:1 NIV.
27. This is taken from Andy Park's book *To Know You More*, pp. 110-111.
28. Taken from Rev. Dr. Paul Davidson's book *Come and Worship*, pp.8-9.
29. See Zephaniah 3:17 NIV.
30. The story about the song and the song "Sweet, Sweet Spirit" written by Doris Akers were taken from *The Handbook to the Baptist Hymnal 1991*, p. 253.
31. Ibid.

Chapter 5: An Invitation to the Throne Room

1. See Revelation chapter 4 NIV.
2. See John 4:24 KJV.
3. See Psalm 32:7.NIV.
4. See Psalm 32:8 NIV.
5. Isaiah 26:3 KJV.

Chapter 6: Creating an Atmosphere for Worship

1. Frances R. Harvergal, "Take My Life and Let It Be Consecrated." *The Baptist Hymnal 1991*, No. 277.
2. See Matthew 6:10 NIV.

3. See 1 Samuel 2:9 KJV.
4. See Psalm 63:8 KJV.
5. See Habakkuk 2:1 NIV.
6. See Exodus 33:15 NIV.
7. See Exodus 33:2 NIV.
8. See Exodus 33:3 NIV.
9. See Matthew 6:21 NIV.
10. See 2 Timothy 3:5 NIV.
11. See Exodus 33:13 NIV.
12. See Exodus 33:14 NIV.
13. See Revelation 4:2 NIV.

Chapter 7: Prepare an Atmosphere of Love

1. See John 13:35 NIV.
2. See John 1:46 NIV.
3. Keith Green is the writer of the song "O Lord You're Beautiful" taken from Hosanna! Music, *Come and Worship*, p. 135.
4. See Colossians 3:16 NIV.
5. See Matthew 6:22 NIV.

Chapter 8: The Fragrance of Intimacy

1. See Psalm 89:20 NIV.
2. See Numbers 16:48 NIV.
3. See Jeremiah 31:3 NIV.
4. See 1 John 4:19 NIV.
5. See John 12:21 NIV.
6. This is line is taken from the song, "This is My Desire" written by
7. See Mark 1:11 NIV.
8. See Mark 9:7 NIV.
9. See Romans 8:15 NIV.
10. See Matthew 18:3-4 NIV.

11. See Galatians 4:6 NIV.
12. See 1 John 3:1 KJV.
13. See Hebrews 1:4 KJV.
14. See Hebrews 1:5 KJV.
15. Kathryn Kuhlman's declaration taken from Benny Hinn's "Atmosphere for Miracle" videotape.
16. See Matthew 22:23 NIV.
17. Jimmy Owens is the writer of the song "Holy Holy." It was taken from *The Baptist Hymnal 1991*, No. 254.

Chapter 9: Precious Tears of Hallowed Moments

1. See Genesis 32:26 NIV.
2. See Luke 7:47 NIV.
3. Luke 13:34 NIV.
4. 2 Samuel 12:13 KJV.
5. The song "This Is My Desire" is written by Reuben Morgan.
6. This song is taken from Israel Houghton's album *Alive in South Africa*; Israel and New Breed.

Chapter 10: Parched Lands and Thirsty Souls

1. See Isaiah 44:3-4 NIV.
2. See Psalm 65:1 NIV.
3. See Joel 2:28-29 NIV.
4. See Luke 24:46-49 NIV.
5. See Amos 4:7-8 NIV.
6. See Deuteronomy 8:7 NIV.
7. See Isaiah 41:17-18 NLT.
8. See 1 Samuel 2:30 NIV.
9. See Acts 2:1-4 NIV.
10. See Acts 2:27 NIV.
11. See Deuteronomy 8:7 NIV.
12. See Jeremiah 33:3 NIV.

Chapter 11: The Season of Great Outpouring

1. See Isaiah 66:8 NASB.
2. See 1 Kings 18:39 NIV.

Chapter 12: Entering the Glory of His Presence

1. See Exodus 33:13 NIV.
2. See Exodus 33:18 NIV.
3. See Isaiah 30:21 NIV.
4. The song "New Degrees of Glory" is one of my compositions taken from the album *The Glory*, 1997, by The Glorious Fountain Ministries.
5. Bob Fitts wrote the song "To Keep Your Lovely Face" taken from the album *Bob Fitts and the Maranatha! Singers*.
6. See 2 Corinthians 3:7-10 NIV.
7. See Acts 5:15-17 NIV.
8. See 2 Corinthians 3:17-18 NIV.
9. See Ezekiel 40:4 NIV.
10. Don Moen, "Take Me Deeper"....
11. See Ezekiel 47:8-10 NLT.
12. See Isaiah 40:4-5 KJV.
13. See 2 Corinthians 2:15-16 Amplified
14. See 2 Timothy 3:15 NIV.
15. See Philippians 3:7 and 10 NIV.
16. See Ecclesiastes 10:10 KJV.
17. See Mark 3:14 KJV.
18. Ibid.
19. Zachariah 4:6[b]
20. See 2 Corinthians 4:6-7 Amplified.

Chapter 13: His Awesome Presence and Glory

1. See Isaiah 6:5 KJV.
2. See Ezekiel 1:28ᵇ KJV.
3. See Revelation 1:17 NIV.
4. The song "Breathe" is written by Clint Brown and is taken from the album *Give God the Highest Praise*.
5. See Psalm 8:3-4 NIV.
6. Stuart K. Hine wrote the all-time classic hymn "How Great Thou Art." This is taken from *The Baptist Hymnal 1991*, No. 10.
7. See Exodus 19:16 NIV.
8. See Exodus 19:18-19 NIV.
9. See Exodus 20:18ᵇ-19 NIV.
10. See Revelation 4:8-11 KJV.
11. The song "Awesome God, Mighty God" is a popular Nigerian praise and worship song. The writer is unknown.
12. See Revelation 22:17 NIV.

Chapter 14: Keeping It Fresh

1. The song "The Steadfast Love of the Lord Never Ceases" is written by Edith McNeil.
2. See John 4:15 NIV.
3. See Jeremiah 2:12-13 NIV.

Chapter 15: Finding the Passion to Worship against All Odds

1. See Psalm 137:1-4 KJV.
2. See John 21:3 NIV.
3. See Proverbs 13: 12 NIV.
4. See John 21:15-17 NIV.
5. See Mark 16:3 NIV.

6. See Job 13:15 NIV.
7. See Psalm 30:5 NASB.
8. See Habakkuk 3:17-19 NIV.
9. The story behind the song "His Eye Is on the Sparrow" was taken from *Amazing Grace: 366 Inspiring Hymn Stories for Daily Devotions*, p.143.
10. The song "I Will Run to You" is written by Darlene Zschech.
11. See Proverbs 13:12 NIV.
12. See Hebrews 13:5 NIV.
13. See 2 Chronicles 20:6 NIV.
14. See Psalm 103:1.
15. See Psalm 42:5 NIV.
16. See Psalm 65:1
17. The song "I Can See Him Working in My Favor" is a popular praise and worship song in Nigeria.
18. The story behind the song "Blessed Assurance" can be found in *The Handbook to the Baptist Hymnal*, p.100.
19. Taken from *The Baptist Hymnal 1991*, No. 334, written by Fanny J. Crosby.
20. Ibid.
21. The song "Let Your Living Water Flow over My Soul" by John Watson.

ABOUT THE AUTHOR

Igho Lewis Yegbeburu is a seminary graduate with a bachelor's degree in Church Music who has been involved in writing, acting, directing, and the producing stage drama. He also has ministerial experience in prison ministry. He is a voice major, songwriter, composer, and arranger. After his seminary training, he served as associate pastor heading the music, discipleship, prayer, and counseling ministries of a dynamic Baptist church with over 1,500 worshipers for four and a half years. In 2005 he obeyed God's leading to resign from this position to dedicate his life to promoting a deeper understanding of true and passionate worship. He is the president of The Glorious Fountain Ministries, an interdenominational ministry committed to promoting worship through music since 1994. His life and ministry are blessed with the grace and presence of God. Igho and his wife, Toyin, are blessed with three adorable children: David, Sharon, and Bliss.

LaVergne, TN USA
29 March 2011
221926LV00001B/33/P